The Concept of Economy in Judaism, Christianity and Islam

Key Concepts in Interreligious Discourses

Edited by
Georges Tamer

Volume 9

The Concept of Economy in Judaism, Christianity and Islam

Edited by
Christoph Böttigheimer and
Wenzel Maximilian Widenka

DE GRUYTER

KCID Editorial Advisory Board:
Prof. Dr. Asma Afsaruddin; Prof. Dr. Nader El-Bizri; Prof. Dr. Christoph Böttigheimer;
Prof. Dr. Patrice Brodeur; Prof. Dr. Elisabeth Gräb-Schmidt; Prof. Dr. Assaad Elias Kattan;
Dr. Ghassan el Masri; PD Dr. Elke Morlok; Prof. Dr. Manfred Pirner; Prof. Dr. Kenneth Seeskin

ISBN 978-3-11-078230-1
e-ISBN (PDF) 978-3-11-078248-6
e-ISBN (EPUB) 978-3-11-078268-4
ISSN 2513-1117

Library of Congress Control Number: 2022943602

Bibliographic information published by the Deutsche Nationalbibliothek
The Deutsche Nationalbibliothek lists this publication in the Deutsche Nationalbibliografie;
detailed bibliographic data are available on the Internet at http://dnb.dnb.de.

© 2023 Walter de Gruyter GmbH, Berlin/Boston
Printing and binding: CPI books GmbH, Leck

www.degruyter.com

Preface

This volume at hand of the book series "Key Concepts in Interreligious Discourses" (KCID) documents the results of a conference which dealt with the concept of "Economy" in Judaism, Christianity and Islam and was held at the Catholic University of Eichstätt-Ingolstadt. The conference was organised by the research unit "Key Concepts in Interreligious Discourses" and, caused by the then ongoing Corona-crisis, took place online on June 17 and 18 2020.

The research unit "Key Concepts in Interreligious Discourses" was jointly run the Friedrich-Alexander-University Erlangen-Nuremberg and the Catholic University Eichstätt-Ingolstadt between June 2018 and June 2021. As the title already implies, the mutual project focused on interreligious discourse. However, it was not about conducting an interreligious dialogue, but rather reflection upon this dialogue, therefor facilitating a theologically well founded interreligious dialogue. For only if every dialogue partner has a clear picture of what is discussed, a dialogue can be conducted reasonably. It was the project's ambition to provide such clarification by examining concepts that are central for Judaism, Christianity and Islam, both historically and in terms of their interdependencies and by setting them in a relation to one another. By reflecting on central ideas and beliefs historically and comparatively, common values and origins, but also differences and contradictions between the three monotheistic religions are to be clearly elaborated. By disclosing key concepts of the three closely interconnected religions: Judaism, Christianity and Islam, a deeper mutual understanding is fostered, prejudices and misunderstandings are counteracted and thus a contribution is made to peaceful interaction based on respect and recognition.

Only through precise knowledge of the central ideas of the foreign as well as of one's own religion a well founded, objective and constructive interreligious understanding can prevail. Conferences at which international experts from the fields of theology, religious studies and philosophy of religion intensively discussed and clarified core religious ideas from the perspective of the three religions served this purpose. Developments within religious history never proceed in isolation; rather, they interpenetrate each other and are mutually dependent. Thus, the research unit "Key Concepts in Interreligious Discourses" pursued fundamental research and aimed at an "archaeology of knowledge" with its comparative conceptual-historical investigations.

Inasmuch as world peace cannot be obtained without religious peace, the project contributed importantly to a peaceful social coexistence and thus corresponds to the obligation that has been newly assigned to the universities in recent decades, namely to engage in social concerns in addition to teaching and research. This is expressed by the term "third mission".

I wish to thank Dr. Wenzel Maximilian Widenka, who not only organised the conference but also edited this volume. In addition to the cooperation partners of the Friedrich-Alexander-University Erlangen-Nuremberg and the de Gruyter publishing house for including this volume in the book series "Key Concepts in Interreligious Discourses", we would like to express our sincere thanks to the third party funders, the Karpos Foundation of the Diocese Eichstätt, Maximilian Bickhoff Foundation and the ProFor Program of the Catholic University Eichstätt-Ingolstadt. Without their support, neither the conference nor the volumes would have been possible.

Christoph Böttigheimer

Table of Contents

Reinhard Cardinal Marx
Foreword —— IX

Moses L. Pava
The Concept of Economy in Judaism —— 1

Andre Habisch
The Concept of ‚Economy' in Christianity —— 43

Rodney Wilson
The Concept of Economy in Islam —— 71

Christoph Böttigheimer and Wenzel M. Widenka
Epilogue —— 129

List of Contributors and Editors —— 141

Index —— 143

Reinhard Cardinal Marx
Foreword

Today we are facing the demanding challenge of globalised goods-, labour- and financial markets as well as an economisation of all spheres of life. Religious communities, too, are not able to fully elude this process of a "economisation of life worlds" (J. Habermas), but they are able to critically reflect on this process and actively shape it; perhaps, where it is necessary, also with a prophetic resistance when there are aberrations and fundamentally wrong positions. First and foremost, they have to emphasize and demand again and again that labour, economy and profit are not ends in themselves, but rather means to serve the well-being of all people. They are means to a fulfilled life. The centre is the human person with his or her dignity, but also responsibility. Since economics is a social science, it is about human agency under the conditions of shortage. Without an ethical perspective, without an orientation towards values, this is impossible

The prophetical religions, the religions of revelation, do not consider the field of economy to be a space free of ethics: Already in the Torah and the prophets of Israel a criticism of social and economic deficiencies based on God's justice can be encountered and not only regarding the people of Israel but already with a universal perspective. Calling for a work-free day in the week, the Shabbat, was in itself revolutionary and has to be defended again and again today. The prophets were also early aware of the close connection between justice and peace between humans and peoples (cf. Ps 85, 11). Jesu's teachings contain criticism of the pure pursuit of profit and too much wealth (cf. Mt 6, 24; Lk 6, 34; Lk 16, 13), because these could destroy the proper relationship with God and between people. Islam, emerged in an environment shaped by trade, has principally a positive approach towards the economic dimension and even towards wealth, but decisively criticises excesses, aberrations and injustices in the social and economic life of these times.

The prophets focus especially on the poor, the weak like widows and orphans, the losers in social and economic events and thus become their advocates because God himself solidarizes with the weak and poor. Judaism, Christianity and Islam demand almsgiving: a mandatory social contribution is actually one of Islam's five pillars of religious practice. However, it is about more than mere charity: the Bible and the Koran focus on "justice", meaning acting according to community that has its model in God himself. Thus, justice became one of the fundamental pillars of Christian social teaching that evolved from the 19th century onwards as an answer to the social question. Christian social teaching is not only concerned with individual agency but also with changes in social, economic, legal and political structures. It is here where I see common challenges and tasks for the religions. The model of a social and at the same time ecologically sustainable market economy could be a comprehensive concept for all religions that is surely to be respelled anew repeatedly. The religions could each contribute their own valuable accents, thus enriching one another. Active advocacy for worker's rights, fair pay, equal opportunities for participation and education, the fight against exploitation, corruption, usury, the waste of resources and destruction of the environment have to be mutual concerns, not only at a national, but also on a global level. Concerning welfare, the religious communities could perhaps cooperate more than they have done so far. Globally, especially regarding climate justice, we are speaking of an orientation towards the "global common good", i.e. the life of all people, indeed the whole creation.

For the benefit of all people, Judaism, Christianity and Islam want to and should provide a critical yet constructive contribution to a positive development of the actually existing national and global economic order, but in doing so they have to set a good example themselves. At the same instance, they will always remind us that a perfectly just and peaceful order on earth always remains an ideal to strive for, and whose fulfilment has an eschatological quantity.

May this collection of essays on economic and social ethics from the perspective of the three abrahamitic religions be a contribution that initiates the necessary reflexions and discussions needed and encourages concrete action.

I want to thank the editorial team and the contributors for the important impulse and the commitment to explore and present the mutual contribution of the religions to the central questions of our time.

Reinhard Cardinal Marx,
Archbishop of Munich and Freising

Moses L. Pava
The Concept of Economy in Judaism

1 The Meaning of Wealth in the Bible

1.1 Covenanting in the Wilderness

Wealth, like life itself, is a sacred gift from God. Ideally, it is to be maintained, equitably shared, and, in turn, handed off to the next generation. Its annual fruits, born only through caring cultivation and the "sweat of your brow" (Genesis 3:19), are to be fully savored and enjoyed, shared, and celebrated, especially among family and community during Sabbath and communal holy days. Wealth is a this-worldly, tangible gift, given by God with the sole purpose of enhancing everyday human experiences. It is a wonderful gift lovingly received in the context of several covenants between God and Israel, most significant of which is the *brit* or covenant at Sinai ("we will do and will listen" Exodus 24:7). The *brit* defines the meaning, responsibilities, and appropriate uses of wealth.

Wealth, as a gift of God, is a central and compelling value in the Mosaic social vision. Wealth satisfies human needs, but it also elevates human dignity and provides the connective tissue of the Israelite community. Wealth, here, is not imagined as part of a utopian society, Eden on earth did not work, but it is promised as an important element toward building a meaningful and sustainable society.

While wealth is a central value, it is just one component in a set of equally compelling *Torah* values. These include freedom (from slavery), loyalty to the covenant, obedience to the law, peace, justice, mercy, charity, kindness, humility, the Israelite people as a whole, tribe, family, memory, love of God, love of the neighbor, and even love of the stranger. And, it is the singular and paramount value of *kedushah* or holiness that weaves together these values into the tapestry of an imagined holy people working, living, and worshipping peacefully in a holy land, in perpetuity. "You shall be to Me a kingdom of priests and a holy nation" (Exodus 19:15). Such a society is to serve as a post-Edenic wholistic model for other nations to emulate, "a light unto the nations" (Isaiah 49:6), a just society that has no knowledge or need of separate economic or, even, political spheres.

Moses L. Pava, Yeshiva University

In the *ḥumash* (Five Books of Moses), human actions related to the acquisition and use of wealth gain exclusive meaning only through the sacred lenses of its many *mitsyot* (commandments) and narratives. To speak of a domain of economic activity and wealth, with its ubiquitous focus on creating ever more efficiencies, faster growth, and more profits, as a separate and stand-alone realm of human behavior, with its own purposes and its own inner logic, distinct from sacred matters, is wholly anachronistic. Ideally every "economic" activity is defined through and gains its meaning exclusively through the shared *brit* or covenant between God and Israel at Sinai. The prohibition on usury among Israelites and the cancellation of debt every seventh year provide good examples of sacred thinking trumping self-interested economic rationality. Another example from Exodus concerning non-economic thinking permeating human exchanges, is the requirement of a lender to return a borrower's pledge before the sun sets. "It is his only clothing, sole covering for his skin. In what else shall he sleep? Therefore, if he cries out to Me, I will pay heed, for I am compassionate" (Exodus 22:26). From the perspective of a modern economist, returning the borrower's pledge daily, is not likely to be the most "efficient" way to ensure repayment on the loan and to the maximize the lender's wealth.

Just as every word and every letter of the Written Torah are considered holy and bursting with many levels of sacred meaning, so, too, every human action is fraught with meaning. According to the Talmudic rabbis not only are the words and letters of the Torah considered holy, but even the spaces and crowns on the letters, contain "heaps and heaps" of meaning. This being the case, it is all the more true that human actions, when properly interpreted, potentially form an integrated mosaic of sacred meaning. Human beings can never fully instantiate God's call to *kedushah* or holiness, but the call itself is permanent.

1.2 What Are the Characteristics of Wealth According to the Covenant?

Examining both the specific *mitsyot* and narratives included in the Pentateuch several normative propositions concerning wealth can be derived.

Wealth is constituted mainly by land and, secondarily, by cattle, but also includes water, precious metals like gold and silver, and other booty conquered in God-sanctioned wars, including slaves, women, and children. Wealth is held in perpetuity by the Israelite nation, by individual tribes, and by families within those tribes, but not 'owned' in the contemporary sense of the word. The laws of inheritance are fixed.

Wealth, within the context of the covenant, carries a wholly positive valence, as can be seen by God's promise to lead the people to a land flowing with milk and honey. Thus, wealth is perceived as nurturing and sweet. Kohelet is certainly correct when he notes that "There is an evil I have observed under the sun...that God sometimes grants a man riches, property, and wealth, so that he does not want for anything his appetite may crave, but God does not permit him to enjoy it" (6:1–2). Further, wealth, and more specifically the land of Israel, not only carries a positive valence, but it is a sacred concept. The land is holy.

Wealth is finite. Its boundaries are permanently defined. Even though wealth is a gift from God it requires human effort to produce its annual return. This is born out in the narrative of the spies, when the Israelites refuse to enter the promised land after receiving their negative report, God punishes the entire generation and vows that not one of them will enter the holy land, with the exceptions of Joshua and Caleb.

Land cannot be sold in perpetuity. Land is returned to its original families during the Jubilee year, occurring once in 50 years. Debts are canceled once in every seven years, during the Sabbatical year and the land must lie fallow. Hebrew slaves are emancipated on the seventh year. Usury is prohibited among Israelites.

Israelites are commanded to guard and to remember the Sabbath and to cease working the land once every seven days, just as God rested on the seventh day, as a reminder and as a celebration that God is the sole creator of the world and redeemer of Israel. The ancient Rabbis taught, "Sanctify the Sabbath by choice meals, by beautiful garments; delight your soul with pleasure and I will reward you for this very pleasure".[1]

Israel is entitled to enjoy its wealth only within the context of the covenant. Dire consequences will result if Israel does not live up to its covenantal responsibilities.

> Take care not to be lured away to serve other gods and bow to them. For the Lord's anger will flare up against you, and He will shut up the skies so that there will be no rain and the ground will not yield its produce; and you will soon perish from the good land that the Lord is assigning you[2]

These responsibilities include numerous rituals and sacrifices, but also include many social responsibilities including several provisions designed specifically to

---

[1] Deuteronomy Raba 3,1
[2] Deuteronomy 11:16–17

protect the poor, widows, orphans, and strangers. Among these laws include the laws of *pe'ah* and gleanings. Leviticus 19:9–10 states as follows:

> When you reap the harvest of your land, you shall not complete your reaping to the corner of your field, and the gleanings of your harvest you shall not take. You shall not pick the undeveloped twigs of your vineyard; and the fallen fruit of your vineyard you shall not gather; *for the poor and the stranger shall you leave them* – I am Hashem, your God.[3] (emphasis added)

Wealth is a positive value and even holy, but greed for more wealth is not good. The narrative of the Israelites requesting meat to satisfy their hunger in the dessert with its negative consequences, "you shall [eat the quail] until it comes out of your nostrils, and it be loathsome unto you," is a permanent reminder that human desires may be infinite but human needs are finite.

With the aid of 20–20 hindsight we look back on the Pentateuch's aspirations, knowing that the covenant, as described above, seemingly violates many of our own contemporary and hard-won notions of morality, seems to neglect certain realities and regularities of human behavior, and thus raises many difficult questions, especially for those advocating a naïve and unproblematic return to the literal Biblical worldview. Several specific issues are worth identifying explicitly.

Slavery, under certain circumstances, is treated as a legitimate form of wealth. Women, taken captive in war, are treated like a form of property for the benefit of the male Israelites. God commands Israel to destroy completely the enemy, seemingly endorsing sacred violence. God's punishments for sinful behavior often seems disproportionate to the violation. Does the human mandate in Genesis to "subdue the earth and have dominion over the fish of the sea and over the birds of the air and over every living thing that moves upon the earth" (Genesis 1:28), give humans too much leeway to do as they please to the earth, as some contemporary environmental critics assert? Is it really a good idea to think of wealth in sacred terms or does this constitute a blurring of the sacred and the profane? Is a society devoid of a separate economic sphere at all realistic to contemplate, especially in a world of ever more specialization?

It is not the purpose of this paper to justify the Biblical worldview in its entirety, or to answer the questions raised above, but two points are worth making here. First, many of these issues and questions were raised during the Talmudic period by the Rabbis themselves. And second, what would be far stranger than a contemporary reader posing critical questions to an ancient text, would be a

---

[3] Leviticus 19:9–10

reader of the Pentateuch who did not have significant questions about many of the characteristics of the covenant. Here my goal has been to identify and briefly summarize some of the major themes on wealth as honestly as possible, keeping normative judgments to a minimum.

I interrogate the text of the Pentateuch, treating it as a single, unified, and sacred document, as the Rabbis in the Talmud treated it. These Rabbis were well aware of the seeming contradictions, critical questions, doubling of narratives, and other literary anomalies identified by academic critics and others over the past two centuries, but they used these oddities in the text creatively to aid in interpreting the Torah's worldview in a way that made it useable for their contemporaries and meaningful to them, given the peculiarities of their historical epoch. Given my own double aims in this study which are 1-to identify myself first as a traditional Jewish insider, and only secondarily as an academic critic, and 2-to contribute in however small a way to an ongoing and ancient conversation centered upon Jewish values as they apply to economic matters, this working assumption, I believe, strengthens my study and its conclusions. What I lose in academic precision, I gain back in Jewish authenticity. In the end, I view my decision to treat the text as a unified whole as a pragmatic choice about methodology, rather than as a truth claim about the Pentateuch.

1.3 Covenantal Living in the Promised Land: The Book of Ruth

> For this commandment which I command thee this day, it is not hidden from thee; neither is it far off, It is not in heaven, that thou shouldest say, Who shall go up for us to heaven, and bring it unto us, that we may hear it, and do it? Neither is it beyond the sea…But the word is very nigh unto thee, in thy mouth, and in thy heart, that thou mayest do it. (Deuteronomy 30 11–14)

What little we know about the actual lived experiences of the Israelites upon entering and conquering the Promised Land is derived mainly from the *Tanaḥ* or Prophets and Writings, and contemporary archeological discoveries. Lived reality in Israel proved to be difficult, dynamic, impossible to predict, and, in some respects, far from the Mosaic vision described above. As in real life, Israel's Biblical history is mainly one of unanticipated events, some brief moments of triumph, but failures and disasters, as well. Great and wise kings emerge, a Temple to God is built, and world-altering prophets, true to Moses's founding vision, take center stage. These prophets offer blunt and memorable criticisms of the wealthy in the name of the covenant, words of hope, dreams of power, fantasies of unity, and provocative visions of wolves and lambs living in harmony, only to be followed by weak and idol-loving leaders, a Temple destroyed, charlatan prophets, and followers dispersed and exiled, only a remnant to return to the land many years later.

All the while Israelite poets compose songs of celebration, thanksgiving, and praise, joyously shouting, "Hallelujah," the echo of which many still hear today. They author, edit, and collect weary dirges, prayers of redemption, books of sad wisdom and useful and practical proverbs, scrolls of human longing and love, a song of songs, and even an accusatory book, describing one man's angry struggles with God and His claims to justice, echoing the original meaning of Israel's founding patriarch's God-given name Israel – "because you have struggled with God" (Genesis 32:28) The once blinding light of the shared covenant between Israel and God flickers, burning brighter and burning dimmer, in turn, but Israel's commitment to the covenant is never completely extinguished over the long and fragile ages. In fact, the covenant, and how to interpret and apply its meanings through actions in each new generation, is usually what we mean when we speak of a "Jewish Tradition" or "Jewish Traditions."

Michael Satlow in his book on Judaism and the economy summarize these ancient texts:

> ...these texts reflect an economy that centered on agriculture. The subject of the Hebrew Bible—the singular "you"—is usually a free, landholding Israelite man who derives his income from farming. Other sources of income are occasionally mentioned in passing (e.g., women's spinning in Proverbs 31:13) but trades, crafts, manufacturing, and banking, among other professions, scarcely appear. Nor does the appearance of a market or market economy happen much until the latest texts of the Hebrew Bible. Whether or not these texts reflected the actual economy, they create an economic ideal centered around land and its periodic redistribution in order to maintain a semblance of equality among Israelite men.[4]

The Book of Ruth, centered on the struggles and triumphs of a Moabite widow who follows her Israelite mother-in-law back to Israel upon the sudden death of her husband, I suggest, provides the best biblical description of a world operating in consonance, at least to the extent possible, with the promises of the covenant and the many propositions identified above. It is a narrative centered upon the land of Israel, how it is to be shared, and who it is to be shared with.

Philip Birnbaum described the Book of Ruth as follows:

> The narrative is one of idyllic beauty. It is the most charming short story in the Bible. It presents a pleasing picture of life in Eretz Yisrael [land of Israel] during the period of the Judges, about two generations before King David. Approximately two-thirds of the narrative is in

---

4 Satlow, Michael, *Judaism and the Economy: A Sourcebook*, London: Routledge, 2019, 15.

dialogue. The principal characters of the story are amiable, courteous, unassuming. They all show how a religious spirit may pervade the conduct of daily life.[5]

In this brief description, however, Birnbaum merely skims the surface of this text.

Bubbling up beneath the idyllic beauty and charm of this all-too familiar, Hebrew-school version of the story, is a much more complex narrative. It includes famine, exile, and the sudden and unexplained deaths of Elimelech, Machlon, and Chilion. It describes the deep depression of Naomi—"Call me Mara for the Lord has made it very bitter for me" (Ruth 1:20) There is Ruth's willingness to surrender her existing relationships to her parents and to her native land and come to a people that she "did not know before" (Ruth 2:11). There is the pure contingency of Ruth who "happened to come upon that part of the field which belonged to Boaz, of the family of Elimelech" (Ruth 2:3).

Further, there is the unexplained kindness and desire on Ruth's part to cling to her mother-in-law. In the most famous and unforgettable lines of the book, we read some of the most passionate words of the Bible:

> Wherever you go, I will go: wherever you stay, I will stay; your people shall be my people, and your God shall be my God; wherever you die, I will die, and there I will be buried. (Ruth 1:16 – 17)

Upon returning to *Beyit Leḥem*, Ruth and Naomi, their needs ignored completely by the townspeople, survive initially by exercising their covenant-sanctioned right to *pe'ah* (the corner of the field that is left available to the least well-off members of the community), the gleanings, and the "fallen fruit of your vineyards," mentioned above. Boaz, who is a near kinsman of Naomi, chooses to interpret these laws as broadly as possible, as Ruth's ambiguous status as a Moabite puts her legal right to this produce and even her membership in the covenantal community, into significant doubt. The instructions in the Torah prohibiting relationships between Israelites and Moabites is stated unequivocally. "…even their [Moabites] tenth generation shall not enter the congregation of Hashem, to eternity…You shall not seek their peace or their welfare, all your days, forever"[6].

Boaz, as the story goes, not only provides Ruth and her mother-in-law with the minimum legal requirements, but responding to Ruth's kindness to Naomi, he provides them with ample sustenance, beyond the letter of the law, or in Rab-

---

[5] Birnbaum, Philip, *Five Megilloth*, New York: Hebrew Publishing Co., 1973, vii.
[6] Deuteronomy 23:7.

binic parlance, Boaz acts *lifnim mishurat hadin*. Boaz's zeal goes so far as to command his young men to purposely let some of the sheaves fall in order to ease the work for Ruth and to allow her to gather a full "ephah of barley" (2:17).

The covenantal laws protecting the stranger to ensure that their basic nutritional necessities are being met, not just in theory but in practice, is here in the Book of Ruth severely tested with an especially hard case, given Ruth's origins in Moab and the Bible's distinctively negative attitude towards this particular people. Perhaps even more significant we also learn from later verses in this text that the laws of land redemption and the levirate marriage are also operating, at least to some extent.

> And Boaz said unto the elders, and unto all the people, you are witnesses, this day, that I have bought all that was Elimelech's, and all that was Chilion's and Mahlon's, of the hand of Naomi. Moreover Ruth the Moabitess, the wife of Mahlon, have I purchased to be my wife, to raise up the name of the dead upon his inheritance that the name of the dead be not cut off from among his brethren, and from the gate of his place: you are witnesses this day. And all the people that were in the gate, and the elders, said, we are witnesses.[7]

The Book of Ruth amplifies our understanding of the Mosaic vision of covenant. Wealth is a central and positive value. It is constituted mainly by land. Land is conceived of as a sacred gift of God, given to the people of Israel. It is not to be sold in perpetuity, but the land is always to return to the original landholding family. Wealth is finite and its boundaries are fixed. Provisions like keeping the corner of the field especially for the poor and indigent are operating effectively. Economic activity is not a separate and distinct sphere of human life, but it is defined exclusively by the Sinai covenant. There is no room for self-interested economic decision making. Human actions matter not just to the actors and their beneficiaries, but human actions gain a kind of cosmic significance as understood against the backdrop of the ongoing covenant between Israel and God. The behavior of Boaz, Naomi, and Ruth is so exemplary in this story that Ruth is blessed with a child named Obed, who became the father of Jesse, the father of King David.

The Book of Ruth not only amplifies our understanding of the meaning of the covenant, but it extends and enlarges our understanding in several distinct and historically important ways. First, we learn from this narrative that the covenant is not a self-interpreting document. There is no such thing. The covenant demands human interpretation at every turn in order to implement it, especially under changing historical circumstances. This point will become even more im-

---

[7] Ruth 4:7–11.

portant as we turn our attention to the Rabbinic period later in the chapter, but it is worthwhile to demonstrate the Biblical precedent for the legitimacy of creative interpretation.

In the case at hand, Boaz, one of the three heroes of the story, chooses to limit the *Torah's* prohibition on marrying Moabites to males only. This is not the most obvious or simplest reading of the original prohibition. Without the Book of Ruth, in fact, an uninformed reader might have reasonably concluded that the Israelites were forbidden to marry both Moabite men *and* women. I suggest, though, that while Boaz's understanding of the Biblical material may not be the simplest one, it is a reading that makes sense of all the words of the original text. Just as importantly, though, Boaz's reading is a better one in the sense that it is a more ethically sensitive one, in that it provides him with an opportunity to implement the Torah's important value of loving the stranger, Ruth being the ultimate outsider. Boaz's choice is later confirmed when the elders explicitly ratify his decision by stating that they are witnesses and that God Himself will consider Ruth like Rachel and like Leah "which two did build the house of Israel…"[8]

A second significant lesson of the Book of Ruth is the recognition on the part of Boaz that while the Torah's laws provide a safety net for the least well-off members of society, for society to flourish and not just to sustain itself, the laws must be implemented with kindness and sensitivity. As stated above, Boaz goes beyond the strict requirements of the law and thus he demonstrates the crucial importance of kindness in bringing the promised covenant to life. One of the significant points here is that even in a God-given context, a social system cannot function without values and in the absence of the human desire for cooperation. Or, to overly simplify, *no kindness, no covenant.*

Third, both Ruth and Naomi demonstrate unequivocally that women are active agents in the context of the covenant, a lesson not obvious in the Pentateuch. For sure, they are not allowed to own land for themselves, nor are the women included among the elders who ratify the laws. Nevertheless, their actions provide an important precedent for future generations.

Finally, the story demonstrates that life remains precarious even in the warm shadow of a living covenant between Israel and God. There are no reasons given for the sudden deaths of Naomi's husband and two sons. It was only by chance that Ruth happened upon Boaz's field. It is worth making the point again that the *ḥumash* is not describing a utopian vision, but a workable one, in the here and now, centered upon a people's relationship with their God, not simply as a philosophical idea, but as the focal point of their entire lives. A world where

---

8 Ruth 4:11.

it makes perfect sense to think of wealth as a sacred gift. It is a this-worldly vision where rewards and punishments are not always directly connected. People prosper and people suffer. There is a rhythm to life. "To everything there is a season, and a time to every purpose under the sun. A time to be born, and a time to die; a time to plant, and a time to gather"[9]

Phillip Birnbaum oversimplifies when he describes the story as charming and the principal characters as amiable, courteous, and unassuming. He is correct, however, perhaps for reasons he himself did not quite consciously comprehend, when he states that "They all show how a religious spirit may pervade the conduct of daily life."

1.4 Kings and the Consolidation of Wealth

> King Solomon excelled all the kings on earth in wealth and in wisdom. All the world came to pay homage to Solomon and to listen to the wisdom with which God had endowed him; and each one would bring his tribute—silver and gold objects, robes, weapons and spices, and mules—in the amount due each year. (I Kings 10: 23 – 25)

Life for the Israelites upon entering the land of Israel was one of gradual change. According to historians, the period from the Exodus until around 975 BCE, was marked by a slow transformation from a pastoral people to an economy based mainly on agriculture. Historian Lewis Paton provides some additional details of daily life for the earliest Israelites:

> In spite of the disturbances which settled life had brought into society, much of the primitive simplicity of manners still remained. The rich and distinguished landowner guarded his sheep and cultivated his fields like his poorest neighbor. The houses of the common people were little better than the tents of the desert. They were mere huts of sun-dried bricks, containing at best only two rooms, and furnished with the utmost simplicity. The rich lived in somewhat larger habitations of stone, whose damp and gloomy interiors were but a slight improvement upon the ancient cave dwellings of Canaan after which they were originally modeled.[10]

Life in Israel during the period of the judges, centered on the family or household. The Israelite diet consisted of barley cakes and milk, regardless of wealth, and meat was consumed only on holidays or family feasts. Members of the same

---

[9] Kohelet 3:1–2.
[10] Paton, Lewis B., "Social, Industrial, and Political Life of Israel Between 950 BCE and 621BCE," *The Biblical World* (1897), 25.

tribe usually settled in the same location, with tribal elders serving as judges and military leaders. National unity during this period was weak, at best, and tribal jealousies were strong.

With the advent of the monarchy around 975 BCE, a nascent political sphere, somewhat independent of the religious authorities, gradually began to emerge. As Solomon created a stable government, internal trade in agricultural products became more common, creating for the first time small agricultural markets. Having said this, it should be emphasized that to think of these markets as even proto-capitalistic would be incorrect. In addition, Israel also engaged in international trade for the first time, importing cedar and fir wood from Lebanon and paying for it with olive oil and wheat. International trade brought with it an increase in wealth beyond landholdings. Just how powerful and wealthy were the Davidic and Solomonic dynasties remains a controversial topic among historians. In any event, the new wealth migrated to a small group of aristocrats and directly to the monarchy and was generally used to purchase luxuries far too expensive for most Israelites, who survived at or slightly above subsistence level. Over time, the monarchy squandered its newly acquired wealth, thus contributing to the break-up of the kingdom into two entities, Judah and Israel.

During the second quarter of the eighth century BCE, there was respite from external domination. The historian Marvin Chaney described this relatively calm period as follows:

> Israel and Judah enjoyed a significant, if relatively brief, respite from big-power domination. They were also at peace with one another, Judah having become a virtual vassal of the larger and more powerful Israel. Both expanded their territories and grew in military power during the long and mostly concurrent reigns of Jeroboam II of Israel (ca. 781–745) and Uzziah of Judah (ca. 781–747).[11]

Chaney points out that despite this respite, peasants, who constituted a majority, often faced a painful decision "What they sowed, they could not eat; what they ate, they could not sow. Current hunger had to be measured against future starvation."

Particularly relevant for this study, given the dire economic situation, Israelite peasants could no longer engage in the long-standing covenantal tradition of loaning one another funds without interest to assist one another in bad years. The only money available was from wealthy landlords, who charged "crushing rates of interest" and often foreclosed on the land and seized it for themselves,

---

[11] Chaney, Marvin, "The Political Economy of Peasant Poverty," *Journal of Religion and Society*, Supplement 10 (2014), 34–60. Here: 35.

thus contributing to the land consolidation and the unequal distribution of wealth. These actions clearly violated the specific terms of the covenant. The Pentateuch's promise of an equitable division of wealth was sacrificed on the altar of self-interest by the monarchy and the small number of wealthy elites surrounding them. It is not even clear to historians whether the Sabbatical Year was observed during this historical period and whether the Jubilee Year was ever implemented at all.[12]

1.5 The Problem with Kings Is You Can't Live with Them and You Can't Live Without Them

The Torah's ambivalence about monarchy is seen both in Deuteronomy and in the Book of Samuel. In Deuteronomy, Chapter 17, the Torah allows the Israelites to choose a king but leaves it up to their discretion.

> If, after you have entered the land that the Lord has assigned to you, and taken possession of it and settled in it, you decide, 'I will set a king over me, as do all the nations about me,' you shall be free to set a king over yourself, one chosen by the Lord your God"[13]

This is the only time in the Pentateuch where covenantal rules are discretionary, rather than obligatory. Further, the Torah's ambiguous attitude towards the monarchy is underscored later by the prophet Samuel in his long complaint to the people about their desire for a king. He reminds them bluntly that they already have a king, stating tersely, "the Lord your God is King"[14].

The final "compromise" here is that the Israelites are allowed a king so long as he always carries a copy of the Torah's teachings with him. Perhaps a bit overoptimistically, Deuteronomy concludes, "Let it remain with him and let him read in it all his life, so that he may learn to revere the Lord his God, to observe faithfully every word of this Torah, as well as these laws"[15].

---

[12] There is evidence from the Book of Maccabee that the Sabbatical year was observed during the Second Temple period, but evidence for the historical implementation of the Jubilee calendar is completely missing. Historian Lee Casperson emphasizes that it is possible that the Israelites did observe the Jubilee year starting during the reign of King Solomon despite the paucity of evidence. Cf. Casperson, Lee, "Sabbatical, Jubilee, and the Temple of Solomon," *Vetus Testamentum* 53 (2003), 286.
[13] Deuteronomy 14–15.
[14] Samuel 12:12.
[15] Samuel 17:19

The Torah's ambivalence about establishing a monarchy is based on the legitimate fear that with a king, a political sphere, with its own inner logic and its own rules, will emerge as a stand-alone domain to compete *against* the covenant, rather than remaining *subordinate* to it. And, in short order, this is exactly what begins to happen. What is less appreciated is a second fear that once the political sphere emerges from the covenant, who or what is to prevent an economic sphere, independent of the covenant, or worse yet, competing against the covenant, to emerge next?

As stated above the kings and their elite supporters began to treat wealth not as a sacred gift from God, but they began to think of wealth as if it was a mere commodity. Thus, the land that constitutes the great majority of the Israelite wealth, begins to lose its holy status, at least, in the minds of the kings and landholders, and perhaps even in the minds of the peasant farmers, as well.

Land is no longer something to be maintained, shared equitably, and handed off from generation to generation. It is not used to elevate the dignity of men and women, but it is used to fill the stomach or to dazzle foreign dignitaries. In the covenantal model, when it was applied with human kindness and interpreted with flexibility, as Boaz did in the time of the judges, wealth served to connect the people to one another and to strengthen the sense of a shared community. Boaz brought in the stranger to share the wealth. Now, wealth has turned into its ugly opposite. Wealth, with its uneven distribution, now divides the people instead of bringing them together.

Within the covenant, wealth was finite and possessed fixed boundaries. Now, the wealthy are beginning to discern a powerful and revolutionary lesson. It is an idea that is almost impossible to forget once it has been learned. With just an ever so slight change in one's mindscape, in the way one makes his or her meaning, it turns out that *wealth can be used to generate more wealth*. It is almost a magical process. When wealth becomes private wealth as opposed to common wealth, one starts thinking of it as a tool to be used for self-interested purposes, and even begins to forget how it was ever possible to imagine wealth as a sacred gift from God. What were we thinking then?

Wealth can now be exploited using instrumental rationality, to earn more wealth, and in turn this wealth can be converted into power to oppress one's fellow Israelites, and so on and on. A vicious circle is created. The outline of a separate and stand-alone economic domain, with its own logic, begins to reveal itself with a vengeance.

Enter the great literary prophets.

1.6 What's a Prophet to Do?

> Prophecy in Israel was not an episode in the life of an individual, but an illumination in the history of the people. A chain of experiences that held together events extending over centuries was an unparalleled fact in the history of mankind...The consistency with the experience and message of his predecessors is such that each prophet regards the revelation he receives as a continuation of what is given to earlier prophets. The Hebrew prophet is not a pioneer; but he hears Him who spoke to Abraham. (Heschel, Abraham Joshua, *The Prophets II*, New York: Harper and Row, 1975, 252)

One of the most important disagreements between kings and prophets is about the nature and the meaning of wealth. The prophets, except perhaps for Samuel, do not call the legitimacy of the monarchy into question, although they may from time to time call the legitimacy of a specific king into question. They have no interest in seeking political office or political power for themselves. They do not castigate the priestly class, although they do deemphasize the priority of the sacrifices.

One of the main complaints on the part of the prophets is the economic oppression of the poor and the condition of the least well-off members of the Israelite society. The prophets are closely watching with alarm as the economic sphere begins to emerge from the strictures of the covenant. And, with its emergence, they intuit the dangerous power of a new way of framing the meaning of wealth, not as sacred, but as an instrumental tool to create more wealth. They try as best they can, with all the rhetorical skills and historical memory that they can muster, to put the cat back into the bag. They insist, with no room for compromise, that wealth is a gift from God and should be treated as such. They view any attempt to detach economics from religion as an unmitigated disaster.

The prophets often speak with anger and ferocity, frequently echoing key texts from Deuteronomy. And, like these Pentateuchal texts, theirs is a this-worldly view, absent, for the most part, any talk of salvation or the perfecting of individual souls. They speak for the people, in the name of God, on behalf of the integrity of the existing covenant between Him and Israel. The Bible presumes that there exists a relatively strong and religious laity who may be open to the prophetic message. Contrary to what many contemporaries assume, the prophets do not invoke a universal morality, nor do they derive their message from natural law or a personal vision of justice. The prophets stand with the people as insiders and teachers who interpret the shared tradition that defines the Israelite people, as they have inherited it. None of them are populists, nor do they seek public approval.

Like all good interpreters, the prophets are intimately familiar with the tradition and in this sense, are entitled to apply it to their contemporary situation.

They reassert the meaning of the original covenant and do not invent anything new.

As the contemporary philosopher Michael Walzer has put it, "Prophetic religion embraced…every aspect of social life. The prophets were (the term is only mildly anachronistic) social critics." He continues:

> The first thing to notice is that the prophetic message depends upon previous messages. It isn't something radically new; the prophet is not the first to find, nor does he make, the morality he expounds. We can detect a certain theological revisionism in some of the later prophets, but none of them presents an entirely original doctrine. For the most part, they disclaim originality— and not only in the obvious sense that they attribute their message to God. It is more important that they continually refer themselves to the epic history and the moral teaching of the Torah: "He hath showed thee, O man, what is good . . ." (Micah 6:8).[16]

The prophet Amos provides an excellent example to illustrate many of these points. He lived during the reigns of Jeroboam II of Israel (ca. 781–745) and Uzziah of Judah (ca. 781–747). He came from a poor village, "a sheep breeder from Tekoa", with no prophets or wealthy landholders in his ancestry. He himself did not want the title of prophet. "I was no prophet…but I was a herdsman, a gatherer of sycamore fruit."[17]

Amos had witnessed firsthand the rise of wealth inequalities. What had once been a covenantal community of freemen was now morphing into something unrecognizable from a traditional perspective. New ways of thinking about wealth and its purposes were popping up and these ideas made little or no sense from how things were supposed to work. "By the eighth century, the years of monarchic rule had produced in and around the court and in the growing cities a new upper class feeding on a new lower class," according to Walzer[18]. Archeological findings support these claims.

Amos reminds the Israelites that the draughts and suffering that they are already undergoing is a result of their sins within the context of the original covenant, as God had already warned them in Deuteronomy. He reminds them of their history and the responsibilities that come with it.

---

16 Walzer, Michael, "Interpretation and Social Criticism," *The Tanner Lectures on Human Values*, Delivered at Harvard University, 1985, downloaded at https://tannerlectures.utah.edu/_documents/a-to-z/w/walzer88.pdf on June 12, 2020, 59.
17 Amos 7:14.
18 Walzer, *Interpretation*, 71.

> Hear this word, O people of Israel, that the Lord has spoken concerning you, concerning the whole family that I brought up from the land of Egypt. You alone have I singled out of all the families of the earth—that is why I will call you to account for all of your iniquities[19].

Among the transgressions of Israel and Judah, Amos observes the extravagance of the winter and summer palaces and explicitly predicts that the "ivory palaces shall be demolished." He accuses the wealthy of defrauding the poor, robbing the needy, selling their fellow Israelites into slavery, taking bribes, detesting "him whose plea is just"[20], subverting "in the gate the cause of the needy"[21], and engaging in sexual improprieties, among other sins.

Amos notes that the wealthy use the "garments taken in pledge" to recline at "the altar of God"[22]. This is a violation of Deuteronomy's requirement, cited above, to return pledges to the poor every evening, but with a wicked twist. As the prophet emphasizes, they do it in a public way and in a sacred place, thus displaying utter contempt for the covenant between Israel and God and indifference to God's compassion for the needy

Instead of enjoying their sacred wealth, earned through caring for the land and hard work, as part of a communal celebration of the Sabbath and festivals, as the covenant imagined it would be, they wish away the new moon festivals and their observance of the Sabbath, so they can get back to selling their grain and wheat at exorbitant prices. In poetic words that still echo through the ages, Amos describes the misbehavior of the wealthy Israelites as if they had embraced an anti-covenant:

> Listen to this, you who devour the needy, annihilating the poor of the land, saying, "If only the new moon were over, so that we could sell grain; the sabbath, so that we could offer wheat for sale, using an ephah that is too small, and a shekel that is too big, tilting a dishonest scale, and selling grain refuse as grain! We will buy the poor for silver, the needy for a pair of sandals."[23]

Compare this to the original covenant at Leviticus 19 and note the similar language.

> You shall not falsify measures of length, weight, or capacity. You shall have an honest balance, honest weights, an honest ephah, and an honest hin. I the LORD am your God who

---

[19] Amos 3: 1–2.
[20] Amos 5:10.
[21] Amos 5:12.
[22] Amos 2:8.
[23] Amos 8:4–6.

freed you from the land of Egypt. You shall faithfully observe all My laws and all My rules: I am the LORD[24].

The message of Amos is grounded not in a universal morality but in the language of the shared covenant. He speaks, like all prophets in the name of the people of Israel on behalf of God, in order to hold the Israelite leadership accountable to the promises that they and their ancestors have made. He is intimately familiar with the specific terms set out in the Pentateuch and refers to the violations of these specific commandments explicitly and often.

Amos is not opposed to religious rituals and the animal sacrifices, but he recognizes that these observances make sense only as a culminating celebration of living a sacred life in a sacred land. When the meaning of wealth has been cut off from its sacred moorings, however, Amos harshly mocks the ensuing religious hypocrisy:

> I loathe, I spurn your festivals, I am not appeased by your solemn assemblies. If you offer Me burnt offering…I will not accept them…Spare me the sound of your hymns and let me not hear the music of your lutes.[25]

The priority is clear. Social justice takes priority over a religious life devoted exclusively to ritual.

With the aid of hindsight, the rise of the monarchy was probably an inevitable step to help to unify the Israelites and to strengthen their ability to defend themselves against their more powerful neighbors and enemies. But monarchy changed Israel's relationship to the covenant permanently by revealing a tiny crack between Israel and God, a gap wide enough to allow Israel just enough room to glimpse faintly a new conception of wealth.

A strict reading of the Pentateuchal covenant views wealth as a static concept. Wealth is equal to land and the boundaries of the land are fixed. This was the view of Boaz in the time of the judges and the view of the Israelite prophets in the time of the kings. It was also the view underlying Amos's criticisms of his fellow Israelites. The economic oppression of the poorest Israelites is a grievous sin in the context of the covenant. But there is a broader concern which the prophets are only just beginning to intuit, if they sense it at all. It is a concern, though, that is subtle and harder to name.

Wealth is ideally viewed as a gift of God, but the Israelites have now recognized through their experiences that it can also be reframed as a kind of tool to

---

[24] Leviticus 35–37.
[25] Amos 5:21.

create more wealth. This dynamic view of wealth is a powerful and generative idea, as history will later prove, but its contours are only dimly understood in the biblical world, if at all. It does raise, though, several questions to begin to ponder: Can the covenant accommodate a dynamic view of wealth? Is this new kind of wealth still to be considered a sacred gift from God? Can wealth be measured? Is there a fixed limit to wealth? Of course, none of these questions are on the minds of the Israelites or their prophets during the period of the monarchy. But with the passage of time all of them will eventually need to be directly engaged.

For most of the biblical period the idea that wealth is something that can be used to create more wealth was inextricably linked to oppressing the poor. Therefore, it was a relatively easy idea to criticize and reject. But it is fair to wonder whether a dynamic view of wealth and the instrumental reasoning underpinning it could somehow be channeled to *improve* society, including enriching its least well-off members. Could wealth be rationally employed to help the poor? And, if so, is it possible that this new wealth – used to improve society and not to oppress the poor – could somehow maintain (or even improve) its sacred status within the covenant?

These questions are decidedly not the questions that Amos or any other prophets raised or thought much about. Nor are these issues of any concern to the Israelite landholders who seem to purposely blind themselves to the hurtful outcomes of their own decisions. But, I suggest, that these questions are ones that the Rabbis and, especially later interpreters of Judaism, consciously or unconsciously, will have to grapple with.

2 Covenant and Wealth in the Period of the Mishna and Talmud

2.1 Judaism's Renewal of the Covenant in the Aftermath of Destruction

In 68 CE, the Roman army, the most powerful in the world at the time, held Jerusalem in its death-grip. The Romans had surrounded the city and rather than attack the well-fortified target, they chose to patiently wait out Jerusalem's inhabitants. The situation inside the besieged city became increasingly desperate. Food was in short supply and hope was even more scarce. The zealots, a group of extremists, literally called the bandits by the Talmud, staged a military coup and took political control of the city. Believing that God would miraculously save them, the zealots destroyed much of the food supply and blockaded the gates of Jerusalem from the inside, preventing anyone from escaping the city. The zealots believed, as a matter of faith, that it was better to die a martyr's death, or even to commit suicide, than to surrender to the vastly superior Roman Army and to give up Jerusalem and the holy Temple.

Yochanan ben Zakkai, universally respected as a teacher of Torah, counseled peace, but realized that this was an impossible dream under the current political circumstances. "How long will you carry on like this and starve everyone to death?" he asked his own nephew, Abba Sikrah, the titular leader of the zealots. But, by now, even Abba Sikrah had lost control of his followers. "What can I do?" He rhetorically responded, "if I tell them anything they will kill me." Realizing that this was his defining moment, Yochanan ben Zakkai, with his nephew's help, devised a plan to escape the city, leaving his coreligionists behind.

He feigned his own death and was carried out in a coffin through the gates of Jerusalem to be buried by his students outside the city limits, as prescribed by Jewish law. Once outside the walls of Jerusalem, he arranged a meeting with Vespasian, the Roman general in charge of the army. During the meeting, he predicted Vespasian's imminent rise to Emperor of Rome. Later, upon receiving news of his elevation, Vespasian granted Yochanan ben Zakkai his modest request to build a Torah Academy in Yavneh, on the Mediterranean coast.

Although Yochanan ben Zakkai *pretended* that he had died in order to escape the Roman siege, his old world would, *in actuality*, be destroyed in just two short years. The Romans breached the walls of Jerusalem in 70 CE. Ultimately, they destroyed the Temple completely, brutally killed thousands, took others as slaves. But like Yochanan ben Zakkai, the rumors of Judaism's death were premature.

Yochanan ben Zakkai's bold innovations at Yavneh would prove to be the seeds for Judaism's renewal, even in the face of seemingly certain destruction. Yochanan ben Zakkai does nothing short of re-envisioning God's relationship to his people. With the Temple in ruins, the sacrificial rites, the centerpiece of religious practice as it was known among the Jewish people until then, were no longer possible. It would seem then the connection between God and Israel had been severed. Grounding his new interpretation in the Prophets, Yochanan ben Zakkai expansively reread the prophet Hosea's statement, "I desired deeds of lovingkindness and not sacrifice," to mean "deeds of lovingkindness on the part of a nation have the atoning power of a sin-offering."

Further, Yochanan ben Zakkai made several specific enactments at Yavneh to promote his new vision. He ruled, for example, that the shofar should now be blown in Yavneh on the Sabbath, a practice that had been restricted before the destruction to Jerusalem only. Similarly, he ruled that the four species should now be taken on all seven days of the holiday of Sukkot, another practice that had been, until then, restricted to Jerusalem. He determined that Jews should continue to eat the bitter herbs on the Passover holiday "to remember the Temple Service," even though the biblical requirement to do so was abrogated with the Temple's destruction. Further, Ben Zakkai established the practices of washing one's hands before eating bread, eating bread with salt, and lighting the Sabbath candles. These practices were designed to emphasize that the table at which one eats his or her meals is like the altar upon which the priests of the past offered sacrifices.

Literally, within months of the destruction of the Temple, he was able to stem the tide of depression among his people, and convincingly offer them a new paradigm. Commenting upon his belief that deeds of lovingkindness can have the same atoning power of sacrifice, Jacob Neusner wrote:

> What Yohanan demanded was that Israel now see, in its humble day-to-day practice, deeds of so grand a dimension as to rival the sacred actions, rites, and gestures of the Temple. If we appreciate the force of powerful emotions aroused by the Temple cult, we may understand how grand a revolution was effected in the simple declaration, so long in coming, that with the destruction of the Temple the realm of the sacred had finally overspread the world. Man must now see in himself, in his selfish motives to be immolated, the noblest sacrifice of all . . . If one wants to do something for God, in a time when the Temple is no more, the offering must be the gift of selfless compassion. The holy altar must be the streets and marketplaces of the world...In the end he accomplished a revolution of the spirit, which has not yet run its course. Yohanan recovered the whole of what was best in ancient teachings and reshaped it for the future.[26]

Underlying this movement, was a new way of experiencing holiness. Here was an alternative perspective, a perspective with antecedents in biblical and rabbinic thinking, but never before so explicitly articulated. Rather than imagining holiness as an external force imposing itself from above upon the Jewish people, such as a father demanding gifts from his children, holiness resides in the ability to find transcendent meaning in everyday actions and rituals, such as washing one's hands before a meal, study of Torah, daily prayers instead of animal sacrifices, eating one's bread at one's own table with family and friends emulating the priests of old, integrity in economic exchanges with one another, and deeds of lovingkindness. In short, Yochanan ben Zakkai rediscovered holiness through living as a community in harmony with the daily, monthly, and annual rhythms of life.

---

26 Neusner, Jacob, *First Century Judaism in Crisis*, Nashville: Abingdon Press, 1975, 173.

"Woe to the children who have been exiled from their father's table"[27] the Talmud states, mourning the destruction of the Temple and its sacrificial rites. This is how the loss was described in the calamitous aftermath of Rome's victory. A way of being in the world, a way of experiencing the holy—*it had been* like children in the presence of their father—had been taken away from the Jewish people. But with the destruction, also came opportunity, growth, and renewal. With the calamity, a new articulation of holiness was explicitly put forward and took hold of the Jewish people.

2.2 Doubling Down on the Covenant's Static Conception of Wealth: The Rabbis Expansive Interpretation of the Biblical Verse: "You Shall Not Wrong One Another"

Concerning those who hoard fruit, lend money for interest, reduce the measures and raise prices, Scripture says, "When will the new moon be gone, that we may sell grain, and the Sabbath that we may set forth corn making the *efah* small and the *shekel* great and falsifying the balance of deceit." And concerning these it is further written in Scripture, "The Lord has sworn by the pride of Jacob. 'Surely I will never forget any of their deeds.'" (Megillah 17b)

Kings have been toppled, priests are without a temple, and prophets no longer have direct access to God. In the aftermath of the Roman destruction of Jerusalem and the loss of political autonomy, Yochanan ben Zakkai is promulgating a new way of experiencing holiness by heightening the experience of everyday life. Everyday actions are infused with a transcendent quality. Despite these epochal events, the scholars of the Mishna (a systematic compilation of Torah laws redacted by Judah the Prince at the beginning of the 3rd century CE) see themselves less as revolutionaries, but as the legitimate heirs and interpreters of the ancient covenant between Israel and God.

As Rabbi Irving Greenberg has put it, "The Rabbis' fundamental theological breakthrough was a kind of secularization insight. The manifest divine presence and activity was being reduced but the covenant was actually being renewed. God had not rejected the Jews, but rather had called them to a new stage of relationship and service"[28]. In this emerging view, the people of Israel, especially

---

[27] Berachot 3a.
[28] Greenberg, Irving, *Perspectives: A Clal Thesis*, New York: The National Jewish Center for Learning and Leadership, 1987, 45.

their teachers, the Rabbis, were now seeing themselves as partners with God rather than as passive agents.

In their upgraded role as partners, these emerging scholars possessed a great deal of autonomy and authority, not as creators of law but as interpreters of it. This was a role that required encyclopedic knowledge of the Written Torah and a great deal of wisdom, sensitivity, and creativity in order to further develop and teach what they were now calling the Oral Torah. This Oral Torah was a set of sacred teachings that had been passed down from to generation to generation since the time of Moses, alongside the Written Torah. It included both laws and narratives and was put into writing and finalized with the redaction of the Mishna and the subsequent redaction of the Babylonian Talmud around 500 CE.

The overarching project of the newly empowered Rabbis was to return to the original covenant and to re-claim its most fundamental principles as their own. They accomplished this task through a scrupulous re-reading of the Written Torah and the generous use of creative interpretive methods. This is true in general, but it is especially true with regards to their attitude towards wealth.

Not unexpectedly, wealth continued to be understood as a sacred gift from God. It continued to be equated primarily with the land of Israel. And, wealth was understood as bounded and fixed, static rather than dynamic. There is no separate political sphere within the jurisdiction of the covenant, and whatever crack had emerged during the period of the kings, has been sealed back up, at least for now. Just as there is no political sphere, there is no stand-alone economic domain either. In fact, just about everything in everyday life is now meant to be permeated with a sense of the sacred and falls under the power and control of the emerging religious leaders, at least in theory.

Jacob Neusner provides one of the clearest descriptions of the Rabbinic attitude towards wealth in the age of the Mishnah. "To the framers of the Mishnah, wealth meant real estate, that alone...Household management satisfies the needs of the household; wealth beyond those needs is meaningless, unnatural".[29] Shopkeepers and money lenders were at best viewed with suspicion. Lending money for profitable investments was not permitted.

> True value (in our sense) lies in the land and produce, not in liquid capital. Seed in the ground yields a crop. Money invested in maintaining the agricultural community from season to season does not. The bias is against not usury but interest, in favor not only of regulating fraud but restricting honest traders.[30]

---

[29] Neusner, Jacob, "Aristotle's Economics and the Mishnah's Economics: The Matter of Wealth and Usury," *Journal of the Study of Judaism* XXI, 1 (1990), 41–59. Here 41.
[30] Neusner, *Aristotle*, 43.

In Neusner's view, the laws of the Mishna are designed to "preserve a perfect, steady-state of wealth." Neusner continues that the Mishna envisions "a perfect balance, proportion, and arrangement of the social order, its goods and services, responsibilities and benefits".[31]

This balance is accomplished, according to Neusner, in several different ways. First, a pervasive principle of the Mishna is that when it comes to economic arrangements, communities are to maintain the traditional practices of their locale. Second, civil penalties are applied to restore the injured party to their previous condition. Third, there is no usury and, in fact, the Mishna expands the Biblical prohibition along several different domains, outlawing exchanges involving any kind of profit. Fourth, and most importantly for the present purposes, all objects possess a true or intrinsic value which the buyer must pay and no more. "In this way the seller does not leave the transaction any richer than when he entered it, or the buyer any poorer".[32] Every economic transaction is conceived of as a form of bartering, even when money is involved.

The most important takeaway from Neusner's description is the deeply conservative aspiration expressed in the Mishna about the concept of wealth. This attitude derives directly from the covenantal conception of wealth described above. When wealth is understood ultimately as a sacred gift from God, presumably there is no need for market mechanisms to allocate scarce resources. In fact, the allocation of resources is the sole prerogative of the Rabbis as the legitimate interpreters of the Torah.

One difference between the Bible and the Mishnah is that in the Mishnah, as economic transactions are becoming more complex, the idea that wealth is bounded and fixed is actually made more explicit than it had originally been in the Biblical period. This is accomplished through a set of arcane laws and regulations to ensure that the old customs are retained, the prohibition on interest is expanded, and that both parties to an exchange always get back exactly what they give.

Regarding the demand that all exchanges must be of equal value, consider, for example, the Mishnah's prohibition of *ona'ah* (literally, wrongdoing). According to the Mishnah, if a vendor sells an item to a purchaser above the "standard price," the purchaser, for a limited time period after the sale, can claim a violation of the laws of *ona'ah*. If the court determines that the selling price is indeed one-sixth greater than the standard price, then the transaction is retroactively canceled, or the excess is returned. Similarly, the vendor is protected, as well,

---

31 Neusner, *Aristotle*, 281.
32 Neusner, *Aristotle*.

meaning that if the purchaser pays one-sixth less than the standard price of the item, the transaction can also be canceled, or the excess is returned to the vendor.

Ideally, the standard price, which was set by communal authorities, is that exact price at which neither party gains nor loses as a result of the exchange. It is not clear to historians precisely how this hypothetical standard price was actually determined in practice, but its theoretical existence is necessitated by the combination of the Mishnaic assumption that total wealth in the economy is fixed and the desire on the part of the Mishnah to ensure that all exchanges are approximately of equal value (one-sixth above or one-sixth below the standard price). If wealth is fixed at a particular level, then it follows directly that all exchanges in the economy must necessarily be zero sum (if one party gains, the other party loses). The only way to ensure that neither party to an exchange is made better or worse off by the exchange is to assume that there is a price (which can be enforced) that will guarantee the equality of the exchange. Although the Mishnah does not describe this standard price as a "just price," based on the above analysis, I believe, using this term is completely appropriate. Similarly, Ephraim Kleiman has defined *ona'ah* as "exploitation through price deceit".[33]

In a sacred society as imagined by the Mishna, the just price set by the communal authorities is the single price that prevents one member of the nation from wronging another member. Any price too high or too low violates the Biblical commandment at Leviticus 25:14: "When you sell property to your neighbor, or buy any from your neighbor, you shall not wrong one another."

The laws related to *ona'ah* are difficult, if not impossible to understand from the perspective of mainstream contemporary economists. This is because the concept of a just price makes no sense when one assumes that all non-coerced exchanges always make both parties to the exchange better off in terms of their own perceived self-interests. Otherwise, why would they have engaged in the exchange in the first place? Economists assume that prices *are set* and *should be set* by the laws of supply and demand, in order to ensure the most efficient allocation of goods and services. The unstated assumption is that prices should be based on a *subjective valuation* of the goods in question.[34]

---

[33] Kleiman, Ephraim, "'Just Price' in Talmudic Literature," *History of Political Economy* 19, 1 (1987), 23–45. Here 25.

[34] Some of these contemporary economists are so certain that their understanding of economics as a value-free science that they re-read and criticize all Mishnaic price regulations as inefficient in outcome and the result of a lack of knowledge on the part of the rabbis of the universal laws of supply and demand. "...Communal controls are forms of price control, and because eco-

In my reading, the concept of a just price makes sense precisely because the aspiration of the Mishna, in line with the Bible's covenantal perspective and the prophetic understanding of it, is that the prices at which economic exchanges take place should ideally be based on Torah values and laws and not subjective valuations. The point is not that the shopkeeper or buyer perceive themselves to be better off after the exchange, but the Mishnah's goal is to protect and to promote the sanctity of the community in the context of the shared covenant, even when it comes to economic exchanges. Market participants are not the ancestors of today's *homo-economicus* but, ideally, they are members of a religious community, not just when it comes to ritual practices, but in all pursuits. There is no separate economic sphere, distinct from the religious one, within which economic exchanges may take place. The importance of this point explains, perhaps, why the Rabbis believed that the very first question you are asked in the world to come is whether you conducted your business with integrity?[35]

2.3 Extending the Scope of the Law to Include Outsiders: Shimon ben Shetach as Moral Exemplar

The Talmud relates the following story that illustrates the idea that all exchanges must be of equal value:

> Shimon ben Shetach was occupied with preparing flax. His disciples said to him, Rabbi, desist. We will buy you an ass, and you will not have to work so hard." They went and bought an ass from an Arab, and a pearl was found on it, whereupon they came to him and said, "From now on you need not work anymore." "Why?" he asked. They said, "We bought you an ass from an Arab and a pearl was found on it." He said to them, "Does its owner know of that?" They answered, "No." He said to them, "Go and give the pearl back to him." "But," they argued, "did not Rabbi Huna, in the name of Rab, say all the world agrees that if you find something which belongs to a heathen, you may keep it?" Their teacher said, "Do you think Shimon ben Shetach is a barbarian? He would prefer to hear the Arab say, 'Blessed be the God of the Jews,' than possess all of the riches of the world...It is written, 'You shall not oppress your neighbor.' Now your neighbor is as

---

nomic science demonstrates price controls to be generally self-defeating, therefore, we shall see that religion and positive (value-free) science may conflict not only in the realm of cosmology or biology, but even in the field of economics and public policy as well" (Makovi, Michael, *Price Controls in Jewish Law*, March 19th, 2017, downloaded at www.poseidon01.ssrn.com). From within the Mishnaic worldview, such a critique, based on subjective valuations, makes little or no sense.

35 Shabbat 31a.

your brother and your brother is as your neighbor. Hence you learn that to rob a Gentile is robbery."[36]

Shimon ben Shetach's students purchased an ass from an Arab in order to lighten his workload and to allow their Rabbi to spend more time learning Torah. The students soon discovered, unbeknownst to the Arab seller, that there was also a valuable pearl, perhaps hidden in a saddle bag. The students were delighted because they could now sell the pearl and with the expected profits their teacher could retire and devote himself full time to the study of Torah. The students viewed this as a case of a lost object and reminded their teacher "all the world" agrees that the law does not require one to return a lost object to a heathen. Shimon ben Shetach, by contrast, will have none of this. In his view, this situation is not about returning lost objects, but it is an economic exchange and thus falls under the laws of *ona'ah,* quoting the Biblical verse from Leviticus, upon which the laws of *ona'ah* are originally based.

Shimon ben Shetach views this as a perfect "teaching moment" to reinforce to his students that one is not allowed to engage in "wrongdoing," when it comes to economic exchanges. He rhetorically asks his students, "Do you think Shimon ben Shetach is a barbarian?" Wealth is not something that one uses to create more wealth, but wealth is viewed as sacred in the context of the covenant. In this case, rather than use the wealth to study Torah full time (a perfectly legitimate use of funds), he can use the wealth to bring the Arab outsider closer to God. Shimon ben Shetach, "would prefer to hear the Arab say, 'Blessed be the God of the Jews,' than possess all of the riches of the world..."

Aspirations always outstrip behavior. Legal rules alone can never ensure that individuals have really understood the meaning and the real purpose of the system of rules in which they are embedded. This is one of the reasons that all of us need to learn from moral exemplars from time to time. In the case at hand, it is important to notice and to point out that Shimon ben Shetach is not just a rule-follower like his students, but through his bold and creative interpretive skills, he is actually broadening the scope of the laws of *ona'ah* not only to include his co-religionists but to include his "heathen" brother. "...your neighbor is as your brother and your brother is as your neighbor. Hence you learn that to rob a Gentile is robbery."

Shimon ben Shetach understands profoundly how difficult it is to create a community in which economic transactions are constrained within religious bounds. This is a perennial problem in the history of the interaction between re-

---

[36] Bava Mezia, ii,5,8c, Jerusalem Talmud

ligion and wealth. If one can engage in wrongdoing against the "other," however that other is defined, is it not likely that soon enough one will find ways to rationalize wrongdoing against one's co-religionists, as well? Just as the Biblical figure of Boaz before him, Shimon ben Shetach understands that for the covenant to function effectively one must seek to actively stretch the borders of the covenant to bring outsiders in (recall Ruth the Moabite) and simultaneously apply the rules with kindness and not just according to the strict letter of the law. Don't forget Shimon ben Shetach could have relied on his students' interpretation of the situation. This Rabbinic narrative illustrates that without the human desire to create a sacred community, i.e. without human values underpinning the covenant, there can be no sacred community. Or, to reiterate a takeaway from the Book of Ruth, no kindness, no covenant.

2.4 The Rabbinic Preference Towards the Working Poor

Consider the case of the "Broken Barrel:"

> Some porters [negligently] broke a barrel of wine belonging to Rabbah son of R. Huna. Thereupon Rabbah seized their garments; so the porters went and complained to Rab. "Return the porters their garments," he ordered. "Is that the law?" Rabbah inquired. "Even so," Rab rejoined, "that thou mayest walk in the way of good men." Their garments having been returned, they observed, "We are poor men, have worked all day, and are in need; are we to get nothing?" "Go and pay them," Rab ordered. "Is that the law?" Rabbah asked. "Even so," was Rab's reply, "and keep the path of righteous."[37]

Human beings need unambiguous signals about the contours of proper legal behavior. On the other hand, the inherent limitations of any rule-based legal code present the possibility for unethical and antisocial activities with the law's approval. Jewish law is consciously aware of this tension inherent in all legal codes. The concept of *lifnim mishurat hadin* (normally translated as beyond the letter of the law), implicitly invoked in the case cited above, is offered as a possible solution.

The facts of the case are as follows: Rabbah hired porters to transport a barrel of wine. In carrying out the assigned task, the porters negligently broke the barrel, and therefore Rabbah's wine was lost. Reading between the lines and teasing out the text (an indispensable task when interpreting a Talmudic case), the porters apparently took Rabah to a local court and "sued" for the re-

---

[37] Bava Metzia 83a

turn of their garments and payment of their daily wages. Rab, acting as the judge or arbitrator, knows of no specific legal ruling that controls the case at hand and obligates Rabbah to return the garments. Certainly, there is no explicit obligation recorded in any legal code requiring payment of the wages. However, Rab determined "even so" Rabbah should (according to some interpretations must) return the garments and pay the employees their wages. The scriptural evidence quoted by Rab suggests that the concept of *lifnim mishurat hadin* is at work here[38].

But why should Rabbah take the economic loss here? As the case states the porters were negligent and this would seem to favor Rabbah's position. Certainly, no modern economist could fully endorse waving one's right to their garments and their wages. After all, what kind of incentives would this create for future porters and other laborers? Nevertheless, Rab believes that the right thing to do is to waive your rights and to allow the porters to go home with their garments, wages, and dignity fully intact.

Please note, that if one is operating in a system where promoting one's self-interest in matters of wealth is the only value in play, then Rab's decision really does not make much sense. However, from the point of view of the Biblical covenant, as interpreted by the Rabbis, wealth is much more than wealth, as economists use the term, and self-interest is not yet recognized as a human value. In fact, one of the purposes of wealth is to elevate human dignity and another is to bring the community together. From this perspective, giving the working poor the advantage in a situation like this does make perfect sense.[39]

Remember the Rabbis are more interested in keeping the covenant and its aspirations alive than the efficiency of the economy. The Rabbis understood well that for the covenant to sustain itself over time, the law will always need a broad set of normative human values and thoughtful judgment to support it. Hence the need to invoke the concept of *lifnim mishurat hadin* – beyond the letter of the law.

---

[38] For a broader discussion on this last point see Pava, Moses L., *Business Ethics: A Jewish Perspective*, New York: Yeshiva University press, 1997, 150.

[39] Similarly, the Rabbis viewed wage disputes between owners and workers as unique, giving the benefit of the doubt to workers over the owners. Generally, in cases of litigation, the imposition of an oath can only free someone from payment. In the case of wage disputes, however, if the employee claims nonpayment of wages and the claim is disputed by the employer, the employee takes an oath and is entitled to receive his wages. The Talmudic discussion raises an important objection. "In what way is the hired laborer different that the Rabbis have instituted for him [the privilege] that he should take the oath and receive [his wages]" (Shebu'ot 45a). For at least some of the Rabbis the answer is based on the relative wealth of owners and workers. "Our Rabbis removed the oath from the householder and imposed it upon the hired laborer for the sake of his [the workers] livelihood."

2.5 Talmudic Accommodation in Contrast to the Prophetic No-Compromise Perspective: The Need for Double Vision

Self-interest is neither a Biblical or Talmudic value or aspiration. Nevertheless, the existence of self-interest, especially in economic matters, is unquestionably a strong motivating force in human behavior. The reality of self-interest is something that the Rabbis accommodated, even if they could never fully endorse it. In this strict sense, the Rabbis were more pragmatic than the prophets ever were. While the prophets, like Amos, adopted a no-compromise position when it came to self-interest, the Rabbis adopted a more flexible attitude. Perhaps the Rabbis learned a lesson from their unbending prophetic ancestors, who despite their eloquent and soaring rhetoric, rarely convinced anyone, at least in their own generations. In fact, the prophet Jonah is the only one to have successfully swayed an entire city to engage in the process of repentance.

Even in Rabbinic stories purposely designed to praise the behavior of those individuals who were able to overcome their own self-interest, like Shimon ben Shetach above, there is the implicit recognition that his students believed that self-interest in economic matters is justified, especially when the profits can be used to enhance one's Torah study. Instrumental reasoning is not an aspirational value – Shimon ben Shetach's students do not ground their argument in self-interest but in law – but it is a very powerful tool to get you what you want. The topic of instrumental reasoning is rarely, if ever, explicitly discussed in Talmudic discourse, but it is a significant concern of the Rabbis, often bubbling up just beneath the surface.

For a good example of how self-interest and instrumental reasoning implicitly permeate the discussion of Talmudic Law, consider the "merchants of Lod." At Bava Metzia 4:3, the Mishnah relates a short anecdote concerning Rabbi Tarfon, one of the most famous Mishnaic Rabbis, and his attempt to re-adjust the laws of *ona'ah*:

> Rabbi Tarfon taught in Lod that *ona'ah* is one-third of the purchase price and not one-sixth... "The merchants of Lod celebrated." But he allowed for retraction of the transaction for the entire day. The merchants of Lod said to him, "Leave us as we were, Rabbi Tarfon," and they reverted to the teaching of the Sages.[40]

The sages allowed a purchaser to contest a transaction if the purchase price was greater than one-sixth of the just price as determined by them, as discussed above. Rabbi Tarfon, who apparently had jurisdiction in Lod, decided to increase

---

[40] Bava Metzia 4:3

the amount of the allowable deviation from one-sixth of the just price to one-third, making it more difficult for the transaction to be contested, after the fact. This change in the law was a cause of celebration to the merchants of Lod. However, the merchants immediately changed their mind, when they learned that the amount of time purchasers would be allowed to contest the transaction was increased to the entire day. Presumably, the merchants did a quick cost-benefit analysis and determined that the benefits of the higher profits per sale would be outweighed by the increased cost due to the increase in the total number of sales that would ultimately be cancelled, as a result of the extra time allotted to the purchaser to contest the transaction. The merchants preferred the original one-sixth profit over one-third profit because they determined, all things considered, that the change was not to their benefit. "Leave us as we were, Rabbi Tarfon."

What is interesting about this case is that, in the end, the new law is rescinded by Rabbi Tarfon. While it is not clear why Rabbi Tarfon proposed the change in the first place, what is clear from this story is that he rescinds it based on the perceived preferences of the merchants.

When all is said and done here, the laws of *ona'ah* are not altered at all. So, one might wonder, what is the point of including this story in the Mishna? I suggest that what this story does convey is the following: While the Rabbis frame these types of exchanges in terms of their own theory of just prices, where every exchange is constrained to be of equal value, as discussed above, at the same time, the Rabbis are well aware that the merchants are viewing the laws of *ona'ah* as a form of price control. From the "self-interested" point of view of the merchants, the difference between the one-sixth (or the one-third price) and the standard price set by the Rabbis is considered as a legitimate form of profit and not as an example of "wrong-doing." The Rabbis can set prices based on their own covenantal understanding of wealth and what it means to them. Further, in their role as teachers, they can promulgate their understanding of the sacred nature of wealth. But what they cannot do is to dictate how merchants frame these transactions. If merchants of Lod view wealth as something to create more wealth, then that is their prerogative. In fact, to achieve their own goals, the Rabbis must necessarily accommodate the perspective of the merchants, just as any living language must accommodate newly emerging concepts. In the story cited above, Rabbi Tarfon and the Mishnah necessarily exhibit a kind of double vision. From a pragmatic perspective, their own view, to be effective at all, must include an understanding of the views of the merchants, however distasteful they may find them.⁴¹

Significantly, the merchants of Lod also exhibit a kind of double vision. From their own accounting, they are in business to make more money. They understand the one-sixth price differential as their hard-won profits and, yet, they accommodate the Rabbis and continue to operate under the jurisdiction of the sages. Their actual behavior does not deviate from the explicit rules as interpreted by the Rabbis. Further, it is likely, that these and other merchants, continue to experience wealth as a sacred gift from God, even as they simultaneously frame wealth as a tool to make more wealth.

2.6 What Does the Price of Pigeons in the Temple Have to Do with Anything?

Despite the centrality of just prices in the Mishnaic teachings, prices in ancient Israel did fluctuate, sometimes substantially, based on the laws of supply and demand. It once happened, for example, that the price of sacrificial pigeons rose sharply in a relatively short period of time. These pigeons were needed by poor women to bring to the Temple after the birth of a child, and the high price caused great difficulty for many of the poor women of Israel. According to Kritut 8a:

> It happened once that the price of two such pigeons went up to a golden dinar. Rabbi Shimon ben Gamliel, the head of the Sanhedrin, then took an oath and said: "I shall not go to bed tonight until the price goes down to a silver dinar."⁴²

---

41 There is a modern analogue to this kind of double vision. Consider a provost of a university who believes that all professors, whether they be liberal arts professors or business professors, should be paid the same salaries based on an appropriate formula. So, for example, whenever a professor is promoted to a higher rank, the professor should receive an additional $10,000 in his or her annual salary. Such a provost is basing his or her understanding of faculty salaries on some version of a theory of just price. This provost, however, in order to attract and maintain quality faculty in business, in a free labor market, will also need to consider how faculty themselves view their salaries.

42 During the period of the Mishna the exchange rate between gold and silver coins was 25:1, although this did fluctuate. See Rabinovich, Laurence J. "Coins and Money in Jewish Law and Literature: A Basic Introduction and Selective Survey" in: Aaron Levine (ed.), *The Oxford Handbook of Judaism and Economic*, Oxford: Oxford University Press, 2010.

Presumably Shimon ben Gamliel, in his august position as head of the Sanhedrin, could have invoked the laws of *ona'ah* or some other form of price control like *hafka'at she'arim,* a Rabbinic enactment that allowed the Rabbis to ensure fair pricing even in cases where *ona'ah* did not apply. This law, known as the law of profiteering in English, was designed to prevent the setting of excessively high prices relative to the customarily accepted ones, even if the purchaser agrees to pay the inflated price. Despite these viable options, Shimon ben Gamliel took a much more drastic approach to solve the problem. Without delay or consultation, he immediately changed the holy sacrificial laws by reducing the number of pigeons women were obligated to bring to the Temple as an offering after child birth. The Talmud continues:

> He went into the *Beth Hamidrash* (study house) and taught: "A woman, even if she gives birth five times, brings only one sacrifice, the rest are no obligation on her." Soon thereafter, the price of the pigeons came down to a half a dinar.[43]

By unilaterally changing the number of pigeons needed for the post-birth sacrificial ritual in the Temple, the demand for such pigeons immediately evaporated and the market collapsed. In fact, Shimon ben Gamliel promised the price would drop to a silver dinar, but actually the price went down even further to a half a dinar.

Merchants were earning obscene profits, according to Shimon ben Gamliel. He was determined to use the power of his office to prevent them from continued profiteering. His bold action demonstrates two points relevant to an understanding of the Mishnaic view of wealth. First, as in the cases cited above, the Rabbis felt a special responsibility to the well-being of the least well-off members of society. In this case, it was the poor mothers who had just given birth who needed their help. Second, despite the Rabbis uneasiness concerning the injustice caused by the laws of supply and demand, they fully understood the mechanism of how prices are determined in a free market, left to its own devices. An exogenous shift down in the demand curve necessarily leads to a drop in the market price. So, while the Rabbis own understanding is that all commodities, including pigeons, possess an intrinsic value, and while they vehemently disapproved of merchants who maximized their business profits, "I shall not go to sleep tonight until the price comes down...", they were willing to use the logic of the market against those merchants who were profiting from the sale of sacrificial animals. They do not approve of the behavior of these merchants, but the chosen solution indicates that they were willing to go a long way towards accommodating the

---

43 Kritut 8

merchants' pattern of thinking and behavior in the service of achieving an equitable public policy outcome. Thus, once again we see an example of double vision.

Shimon ben Gamliel goes down in history as a champion of just price theory, but it should be noted that he himself employs the same type of instrumental logic that the merchants use. An alternative to instrumental thinking is the more emblematic Rabbinic process of interpreting and teaching sacred texts. Typically, the hope is that through the intensive study and practice of Torah, a culture of faith will emerge where the reward of doing a mitzvah is the mitzvah itself. "Do not be like servants who serve the master in the expectation of receiving a reward but be like servants who serve the master without the expectation of receiving a reward..."[44]. Shimon ben Gamliel is doing everything in his power to prevent a distinct economic sphere from emerging outside the parameters of the covenant, in order to protect the idea of sacred wealth. But ironically, he is employing the very same tools that the merchants use to pursue their own self-interests and so in this sense perhaps he is getting his hands dirty.

2.7 Hillel's *Prosbol* as an Accommodation to Market Realities

Rabbi Tarfon and Shimon ben Gamliel both employ a double vision in order to maintain the principles of the covenant and, at the same time, to accommodate the powerful motivation on the part of merchants to use their existing wealth to create even more wealth for themselves. Another example of double vision in the area of economics is Hillel's innovative *prosbol*. By the first century BCE, it was becoming more difficult for the Israelites to borrow money from one another. Given the Bible's demand that all debts are canceled in the seventh year, self-interested creditors became more hesitant to lend money, afraid that they would not be repaid before the Sabbatical year and the automatic cancellation of the debt.

The required cancellation of loans during the seventh year created a tremendous barrier to making funds available to the needy. Hillel's solution is recorded in the Talmudic tractate of Gittin (36a–36b). The *prosbol* is a legal document which allows the lender and borrower to circumvent the cancellation of the debt. According to the Talmud, the text of the *prosbol* read as follows: "I hand over to you, So-and-so, the judges in such-and-such a place, [my bond], so that I may be able to recover any money owning to me for So-and-so at any

---

[44] Pirkei Avot 1:3.

time I shall desire." The loophole underlying the *prosbol* is that while an individual is prohibited from collecting on the loan at the end of the seventh year, the rabbinical court is not. Therefore, the court could collect the funds from the borrower and turn them over to the lender. The effect, of course, was to nullify the law, without violating it.

Hillel's *prosbol* was an innovation but not an invention. Importantly, his interpretation was firmly grounded in the Biblical text. According to the Sifre, the seemingly superfluous phrase at Deuteronomy 15:3, "but whatsoever of thine is with thy brother thy hand shall release," suggested that contrary to the verse, if the bond was in the hands of the rabbinical court, no release was required. Further, the institution of the *prosbol* can be understood as a fulfillment of Deuteronomy 15:9, where the Bible itself warns:

> Beware that there be not a base thought in thy heart, saying: "The seventh year, the year of release, is at hand," and thine eye be evil against thy needy brother, and thou give him [i.e. lend him] naught; and he cry unto the Eternal One against thee, and it be sin in thee.[45]

This verse might have been interpreted only as a warning addressed to the individual, and therefore its fulfillment or nonfulfillment would have been appropriately left to the discretion of each member of the community. However, Hillel creatively chose to read it as an exhortation to the community. The community has a responsibility to ensure that the needs of the poor are being met. Through the institution of the *prosbol,* Hillel, given the reality of the laws of supply and demand, provided a better and more ethically sensitive reading of the Biblical material.[46]

2.8 Sacred Compromise as a Pragmatic Approach to Maintaining the Concept of Sacred Wealth During the Talmudic Period and Beyond

The fundamental goal for Hillel and all of the Rabbis of the Mishna is to maintain the concept of wealth as a sacred gift from God. This is an idea that they

---

45 Deuteronomy 15:9
46 Eliezer Berkovits in his penetrating book, *Not in Heaven: The Nature and Function of Halakha*, catalogues numerous additional instances where Jewish law in interpreted in such a way as to promote economic welfare and thus ensure the continued viability of the community. Cf. Berkowitz, Eliezer, *Not in Heaven: The Nature and Function of Halakha*, New York: Ktav, 1983. Cf. Pava, *Business Ethics*, 133–135, for further discussion.

have inherited from the Biblical conception of wealth, as articulated in the covenant, and one that they view as critical and non-negotiable to the sustainability of the Jewish people over time. To do so, on the one hand, the Rabbis needed to recognize and to understand the emergence of self-interested behavior on the part of economic agents and the rudiments of the laws of supply and demand. On the other hand, they needed to strictly circumscribe such instrumental behavior within tolerable religious bounds. In order to hold onto to some notion of wealth as sacred, the Rabbis needed to maintain their own control over market exchanges and not allow a separate economic domain to break out beyond the confines of the covenant. They needed to do so, even if this meant accommodating merchants to earn up to one-sixth profits (at least from the merchants point of view) and requiring the Rabbis to nullify the Biblical law that requires the cancellation of debt in the Sabbatical year through the innovative interpretation of the covenant.

In other words, the goal of viewing wealth in sacred terms required a great deal of sacred compromise. This is true from the point of view of the Rabbis and it is also true from the perspective of the merchants, who at the end of the day will sometimes need to curtail their profits and their own self-interested behavior to remain within the covenantal framework as interpreted by the Rabbis.

While this is not a perfect solution to the problem of remaining true to covenantal principles and accommodating the reality of self-interested behavior on the part of merchants and landowners, there is no perfect solution. The method and enormous power of creative interpretation does provide a *good enough* solution in the sense that it has functioned during the period of the Talmud and well beyond, even to the present day in many traditional Jewish communities, to ensure the sustainability of the covenantal community over time, thriving in some periods and merely surviving in others. And, to the extent that merchants continue to abide by the broad boundaries set up by the Rabbis, even as Rabbinical authority has diminished in many communities and in many time periods, they too may, through their desire to voluntarily uphold the covenant, experience wealth as a sacred gift from God to a greater or lesser degree.

3 Post Traditional Societies and Beyond

Post traditional societies are fragmented. Both politics and economics have emerged as autonomous or nearly autonomous domains of action. It is hard if not impossible to function in today's world in either of these domains without the explicit use of instrumental reasoning. Among other things this means that individuals are encouraged to choose their own actions to promote their own interests, as they perceive those interests, to maximize their own future happiness and their own wealth. This change did not happen overnight in 1776 when Adam Smith published his famous treatise on the wealth of nations, although his careful arguments did legitimize the notion of self-interest in a convincing way, at least from the unique moral perspective now known as utilitarianism. Rather it was a gradual change, as documented above, beginning as far back as the period of Biblical monarchy and extending into the Rabbinic period.

The internal logic of the economic sphere has proved to be a powerful force in society. It turns out that wealth, conceived of as a commodity, can be used to create more wealth beyond even the wildest imaginings of traditional thinking. And, further, this explosion of wealth is associated with positive breakthroughs in a broad array of areas including: life expectancies, health, food, technology, communication, education, safety, measures of happiness, and even human rights. These findings present serious challenges to those who have conceived of wealth and wealth creation as a zero-sum game and those who assume that too much wealth is always and only oppressive. Having said this, however, it should also be noted that such "progress" has not come without its own costs. Consider the following:

1-Income and wealth inequalities have risen to unprecedented levels, 2-climate change caused by the burning of fossil fuels has disrupted human and animal environments in dangerous and threatening ways, 3-racism and sexism continue to haunt us despite efforts to reduce them, and 4-government institutions and agencies have been corrupted by lobbyists, political donors, and other nefarious actors, making it almost impossible to promote wise public policies, even when it comes to a pandemic.

Judaism, not unexpectedly in an age of fragmentation, has responded to these epochal changes in different ways. Traditionalists, for example, continue to assume that the role of Rabbinic authority in economic matters has not changed in any meaningful way. Economic players in traditional Jewish communities across the world continue to seek authoritative guidance from their Rabbis in matters economic, at least in theory. For these traditionalists, the notion of a post traditional Judaism is an oxymoron.

From the traditionalists' perspective, the final verdict on the meaning of economic activity is determined exclusively by the "declaration" of Jewish Law and custom. The covenant between God and Israel is interpreted in much the same way as it was in Talmudic times and one holds on fast to the aspiration of wealth as a sacred gift from God.

The economic roles that traditionalists can take on in a modern economy may be truncated or even severely truncated, as not every job can easily be translated into Jewish terms, but the benefit for the traditionalists is the attractive promise of potentially living a life of complete integrity within an all-encompassing Jewish world of meaning.

A second group, let us call them the integrationists, have adopted a more modern approach to conceptualizing the relationship between Judaism and economics. The late Rabbi Jonathan Sacks, former Chief Rabbi of Great Britain and the 2016 winner of the Templeton Prize, was perhaps the most well-known and leading advocate of the integrationist position in Judaism.

In Sacks' view, capitalism is not justified in specifically Jewish or religious terms, but its worth is grounded in a purely utilitarian calculus. Sacks writes approvingly that "The market economy has generated more real wealth, eliminated more poverty and liberated more human creativity than any other economic system."[47] If there is a problem here, "The fault is not with the market but with the idea that the market alone is all we need."

For Sacks, improving the health of capitalism is not an economic question at all and it is certainly too important a task to leave to business managers. Rather, the task is a moral one and needs to be imposed upon business from the outside. For the traditionalists discussed above, market activity is translated into Jewish meaning, here, for the integrationists, Jewish values, external to the practice of business, fully determine the boundaries of legitimate and just market activities.

For modern Jews, the integrationist position provides the license to participate fully in the contemporary economy as investment bankers, chief executive officers, managers, employees, advertisers, accountants, lawyers, investors, manufacturers, etc. Nevertheless, there is a cost incurred, if often unseen by the integrationists and their followers. Much of one's life, for some between 40 and 60 hours per week, is now experienced as distinct from the authentic Jewish meanings experienced by the traditionalists and by the integrationists in their private lives.

One way of thinking about this is that the scope of the covenant has shrunk and further this means that it is now almost impossible to conceive of wealth as a sacred gift from God. In fact, now, wealth is merely a commodity.

For a third approach, let us call them the constructivists, there is a desire to re-imagine business organizations, not only as producers of wealth, but as a place for pursuing higher purposes and meanings. For constructivists, justifying capitalism as Sacks does, only in terms of its ability to create the greatest wealth at the least cost is no longer sufficient. *How* we create wealth inside the black box of business is becoming as important as *how much* wealth we create.

---

47 Sacks, Jonathan, *Morals: The One Thing Markets Do Not Make*. http://rabbisacks.org/morals-the-one-thing-markets-do-not-make-published-in-the-times/. Accessed 1 July 2019.

For Jewish business ethicists embracing the constructivist perspective, the goal of a Jewish business ethics is to self-consciously explore ways of building into business from the ground up a broader set of values – Jewish and otherwise – beyond the efficient production of wealth. Business is no longer seen as a neutral and technocratic practice, but it is better thought of as a fully human enterprise. The covenant is put into dialogue with the economic domain.

Unlike integrationists, from this perspective Jewish voices participate fully in ongoing and pluralistic dialogues and no longer see themselves as external umpires, arriving on the scene with Jewish and business rulebooks already in hand. Jewish business ethicists no longer view their job primarily as discovering a set of pre-existing constraints and then applying them to the practice of wealth creation, but they view their task as part of a larger creative and constructive project, requiring them to get their hands dirty with the details and particularities of business. For this project to get off the ground participants need to be pragmatic, flexible, imaginative, and willing to compromise with others, something that traditionalists and integrationists have trouble accepting.

The constructivists continue to experience the transcendent and holy quality of one's private religious practices as do the traditionalists and integrationists, but now such sacred experiences *also* serve as a paradigm case of human meaning. Purely human practices, including wealth creation in all of its varieties may provide a secular, temporary, this-worldly, and finite analogue, a taste of something similar enough to the sacred to call it meaningful, without causing undue confusion.

The ability to instantiate one's values, to give at least temporary reality to one's deepest hopes and concerns in the real world through institutionalizing those values and concerns in businesses designed with higher purposes in mind, is an experience that at its best may potentially remind one of more profound and more permanent experiences. Using religious vocabulary metaphorically to communicate about and to enhance the significance of purely human interactions is a practically and pragmatically useful phenomenon. As long as one continues to remember that business covenants are only *like* religious ones, that kindness in business is *not precisely* what Jewish kindness expects in more purely religious contexts, and as long as one knows that Sabbath Consciousness is just *a reflection* of the experience of observing the traditional rules of the Sabbath, purposefully choosing to secularize such concepts may not harm them at all and may, in turn, actually deepen one's religious appreciation for them in the long run.

Integrationists casually assume that market exchanges always have a tendency to crowd out other kinds of exchanges, hence the need for the Jewish ethics police. Constructivists, however, harbor the hope that this is not quite right.

More thoughtful and conscious organizations designed with ethics built in from the ground up might potentially provide an environment where more market exchanges can actually broaden the playing field and allow for and encourage more meaningful human exchanges, at the same time.

Finally, for the constructivists, the need to search for meaning in organizations may be so great, their faith in the polysemic character of Jewish values so firm, and their belief in the strength and integrity of Torah so stable that constructivism is experienced as a natural and obvious next stage in the development of their Jewish identity rather than seeing it as a risky choice, at all.

4 Conclusion

The long history of Judaism and economics is fundamentally a question of how best to interpret the Biblical covenant between God and Israel under profoundly changing circumstances, including changes to the very definition of wealth. This chapter has examined the period of the prophets, the rabbinic epoch, and three post traditional responses in today's fragmented world. For those that continue to insist on the primacy of the covenant, the consensus is that it is still worth imagining what kind of world is it that we have a responsibility to create together, if we want to believe that wealth remains, or at least is treated, as if it is a sacred gift from God. The Jewish faith today is that we can still develop good enough answers to keep this story going.

Bibliography

Berkowitz, Eliezer, *Not in Heaven: The Nature and Function of Halakha*, New York: Ktav, 1983.
Birnbaum, Philip, *Five Megilloth*, New York: Hebrew Publishing Co., 1973.
Casperson, Lee, "Sabbatical, Jubilee, and the Temple of Solomon," *Vetus Testamentum* 53, (2003), 283–296.
Chaney, Marvin, "The Political Economy of Peasant Poverty," *Journal of Religion and Society*, Supplement 10 (2014), 34–60.
Greenberg, Irving, *Perspectives: A Clal Thesis*, The National Jewish Center for Learning and Leadership, New York, 1987.
Heschel, Abraham Joshua, *The Prophets II*, New York: Harper and Row, 1975.
Kleiman, Ephraim, "'Just Price' in Talmudic Literature," *History of Political Economy* 19, 1 (1987), 23–45.
Makovi, Michael, *New Wine in Old Flasks: The Just Price and Price-Controls in Jewish Law*, MPRA Paper No. 69119, 2016.
Neusner, Jacob, *First Century Judaism in Crisis*, Nashville: Abingdon Press, 1975.

Neusner, Jacob, "Aristotle's Economics and the Mishnah's Economics: The Matter of Wealth and Usury," *Journal of the Study of Judaism* XXI, 1 (1990), 41–59.

Neusner, Jacob, *The Theology of the Oral Torah*, Montreal: McGill-Queens University Press, 1999.

Paton, Lewis B., "Social, Industrial, and Political Life of Israel between 950 BCE and 621BCE," *The Biblical World* (1897), 24–32.

Pava, Moses L., *Business Ethics: A Jewish Perspective*, New York: Yeshiva University Press, 1997.

Rabinovich, Laurence J., "Coins and Money in Jewish Law and Literature: A Basic Introduction and Selective Survey," in: Aaron Levine (ed.), *The Oxford Handbook of Judaism and Economic*, Oxford: Oxford University Press, 2010, 564–583.

Satlow, Michael, *Judaism and the Economy: A Sourcebook*, London: Routledge, 2019.

Sacks, Jonathan, *Morals: The One Thing Markets Do Not Make*, http://rabbisacks.org/morals-the-one-thing-markets-do-not-make-published-in-the-times/ . Accessed 1 July 2019.

Walzer, Michael, "Interpretation and Social Criticism," *The Tanner Lectures on Human Values*, Delivered at Harvard University, 1985, downloaded at https://tannerlectures.utah.edu/_documents/a-to-z/w/walzer88.pdf on June 12, 2020.

Suggestions for Further Reading:

Dembitz, Lewis N., "Ona'ah," https://www.jewishencyclopedia.com/articles/11707-ona-ah.

Friedman, Hershey H. The Impact of Jewish Values on Marketing and Business Practices. https://aish-international.com/impact-jewish-values-marketing-business-practices/. 2017. Accessed 13 March 2020.

Levine, Aaron / Pava, Moses, *Jewish Business Ethics: The Firm and Its Stakeholders*, Northvale, NJ: Jason Aronson Inc, 1999.

Levine, Aaron, *Free Enterprise and Jewish Law: Aspects of Jewish Business Ethics*, Jersey City, NH: Ktav Publishing, 1979

Levine, Aaron, *Economics and Jewish Law: Halakhic Perspectives*. Jersey City, NH: Ktav Publishing, 1987.

Levine, Aaron, *Economic Public Policy and Jewish Law*, Jersey City, NH: Ktav Publishing, 1993.

Levine, Aaron, *Case Studies in Jewish Business Ethics*. Jersey City, NH: Ktav Publishing, 1999

Neusner, Jacob, *Economics of the Mishnah*, Chicago: University of Chicago Press, 1990.

Pava, Moses L., "The Talmudic Concept of 'Beyond the Letter of the Law': Relevance to Business Social Responsibilities", *Journal of Business Ethics* 15, 9 (1996), 941–950.

Pava, Moses L., *Leading with Meaning: Using Covenantal Leadership to Build a Better Organization*, New York: Palgrave, 2001.

Pava, Moses L., *Jewish Ethics in a Post-Madoff World: A Case of Optimism*, New York: Palgrave, 2001.

Pava, Moses L., "Jewish Ethics," in: Kolb, Robert W. (ed.), *The SAGE Encyclopedia of Business Ethics and Society*, Thousand Oaks, CA: Sage Publications, 2018, 1965–1968.

Pava, Moses L., *Jewish Ethics as Dialogue. Using Spiritual Language to Build a Better World*, New York: Palgrave, 2009.

Pava, Moses L., *Business Ethics. A Jewish Perspective (Library of Jewish Law & Ethics)*, Jersey City, NJ: Ktav Publishing, 1997.

Rakover, Nahum, *Ethics in the Market Place: A Jewish Perspective*, Jerusalem: Library of Jewish Law, 2000.

Rosenfeld, Ben-Zion and Menirav, Joseph, "Methods of Pricing and Price Regulation in Roman Palestine in the Third and Fourth Centuries," *Journal of the American Oriental Society*, 121, 3 (2001), 351–369.

Sacks, Jonathan, Tikkun Olam: "Orthodoxy's Responsibility to Perfect G-d's World." https://advocacy.ou.org/tikkun-olam-orthodoxys-responsibility-to-perfect-g-ds-world/. 1997. Accessed 1 July 2019.

Tamari, Meir, "The Challenge of Wealth: 'Jewish Business Ethics,'" *Business Ethics Quarterly* 7, 2 (1997). 45–56.

Wurzburger, Walter, "Covenantal Morality in Business," in: Aaron Levine / Moses Pava, *Jewish Business Ethics: The Firm and Its Stakeholders*, 27–44, Northvale, NJ: Jason Aronson Inc., 1999.

Andre Habisch
The Concept of ‚Economy' in Christianity

1 Introduction: Theological Critique of Economy/ Economics in Christian theology

Economy, economic perspectives, analyses, discussions, and interventions etc. play a crucial role in the contemporary social world. Many Christian theologians find this a regrettable fact. For them, especially during the last decades, *the* Economy and its perceived imperatives have become synonymous with social dismantling, practices of human instrumentalization, exploitation of workers and welfare cuts in the social and cultural sector etc. Apparently, in the name of economic arguments, an increase in poverty and neglect of the needy was tolerated or even actively encouraged. For example, the Thatcher/ Reagan liberalization reforms in the US/ UK, but also the so-called 'Washington consensus' – impacting developmental aid, international monetary relations etc. – were perceived as driven by 'the economy' and in general contrast to Christian values.

In a historical perspective, Christian tradition is of crucial importance for both: the development of the contemporary concept of Economy, Economic development, and Economics as its academic subject – as well as for its critique by theologians, philosophers, social scientists etc. Thereby, the dualism between Economy and its critique broadly corresponds with intercultural and international differences as well. More precisely, the Anglo-Saxon tradition with its liberal, utilitarian, and individualistic tendencies represented the most important driver of Economic theory and policies, while central and southern European intellectual and political traditions opposed them and called for a different orientation. If we break this down on a confessional level – following the important religious Sociologist Max Weber in this respect – there were mostly Protestant reformist and Calvinist groups to promote the former while many Catholic and Conservative Lutheran thought leaders formulated a conservative opposition.

Antagonisms of that kind often indicate conceptual flaws and misunderstandings of a concept. Hence, a more detailed and careful reconstruction of the multifaceted history of 'Economy' seems necessary to rationalize the discussion. In the following chapter, we show how different socio-economic production regimes corresponded with different theoretical conceptualizations of 'Econo-

Andre Habisch, Catholic University, Eichstätt-Ingolstadt

https://doi.org/10.1515/9783110782486-004

my'. For that purpose, we start with the emergence of the concept in the Greek Philosophy.

2 Historical Development of Christian Economical Thought

2.1 Economy in Greek Philosophy (*oikonomía*)

The historical origins of the concept of economics are much older than Christianity, dating back to the 4th century BC. When the Christian religion emerged, Greek language, philosophy and culture still dominated the Roman Empire and formed the main point of reference for philosophical and theoretical concepts. Consequently, many documents of the religious sacred writings also show a strong influence of Greek philosophy – something that is also evident regarding the concept of Economy. It was the Greek philosopher Aristotle (384–322 BC), or one of his disciples, who authored the most influential early book on 'the Economies' (Plural). It defines *oikonomía* from Greek *oikos* – "household" and *némonai* – "manage". Thus, *oikonomía* signifies the management of a household or of household affairs. More precisely, the basic meaning of the word is focused on "handling", "management" or more literally "housekeeping" of a thing. The meaning is not only positive-descriptive but entails a normative meaning as well: the goal is a good or prudent (as opposed to a bad) treatment of the matter in question.

To grasp the meaning of that concept correctly, however, a contemporary reader should consider the high importance Aristotle places on the role of practical excellence, the ability to apply relevant theoretical concepts in an adequate and situation-specific way. A professional Economist should therefore become aware of relevant situational circumstances and deal with them in an adequate way. Aristotle opposed the concept of his teacher Plato, here, who had emphasized the role of theoretical knowledge thereby ultimately calling for a strong social role of Philosopher-kings. In contrast, Aristotle prioritized practical wisdom ('*phronesis*') over theoretical knowledge ('*episteme*') only. While a mere conceptual thinker could still fail dramatically, being able to apply theoretical concepts correctly in a historically given situation does indeed represent an important part of true mastership. Hence, Aristotle criticized a 'deductive' approach towards Economy, which unilaterally refers to fixed theoretical 'laws' resulting in 'one-fits-all' concepts. Economizing must rather start with a careful analysis of the status quo as well as a reflection on long-term consequences of own decisions.

In contemporary English, 'customizing' a good or service towards individual preferences expresses well what is at stake. The professional Economist must customize abstract economic concepts to the situation of his family.

Thereby, in contrast to the modern term of 'Economy', '*oikonomía*' never refers to the totality of all structures and processes of production, distribution and consumption of goods and services within a national or regional economy. It rather only designates planned economic activity of a single person or an organized association of persons, usually the individual household. More precisely, it includes the production, handling and distribution of goods and services for life. In a modern sense, *oikonomía* refers more to the research object of business/organizational studies than to the research object of modern economics: the Economy as a whole.

Aristotle's philosophy remained the most important point of reference not only in antiquity, i.e. until the collapse of the Roman Empire in the Migration Period and the early Middle Ages. It also influenced Christian economic thought for centuries. Aristotle was able to play this role due to the reception of his work by medieval authors such as Thomas Aquinas (1225–1247). In his "*Summa Theologiae*", the medieval Doctor of the Church drew heavily on the – then just rediscovered – work of the Greek (Thomas simply called him "the philosopher"). For an essay dealing with the concept of economy in Christianity, it is therefore necessary to carefully evaluate the *oikonomía*.

The concept starts with the (male) owner of a piece of arable land and makes recommendations how to life a fulfilled live, thereby thriving for economic well-being and happiness. The author enfolds his discourse concerning this topic by applying what we today would call a 'stakeholder approach' – in the sense that he describes the relations with the most important partner-persons needed to reach these goals: the wife, the children, the slaves helping him to cultivate the land, the neighbors etc. All these people should be treated with respect – but also closely guarded. It remains the duty of a true economist-owner to supervise every aspect of his household, for no one will do this as conscientiously as he himself as owner. The main occupation of our economist is to cultivate his land in the sense of growing produce that can be sold in the market. In doing so, he should remember that expenditure must not exceed his income and that he must participate in the flow of money in the economy. Following this, the (second) book describes various economic activities and investments that are made in today's economy.

A very important aspect here is the difference between Economics and 'chrematistics', which subsequently influenced medieval thought until the Age of Enlightenment. While Economics as housekeeping is focused on balancing income and expenses (thereby assuring the 'adequate' standard of living), Chrematistics is striving to accumulate more and more money – and ultimately the creation of wealth. For Aristotle, a Chrematistic mindset to accumulate money and profit is unnatural and hampers the Human development of the person pursuing it; it is rather connected with the profession of the traders or lenders, i.e. persons, which in the perspective of an antique author are not productive. Buying produced goods in one place and selling it for a higher price elsewhere, or lending money for payment of interest: both represent economic activities, which do not seem to add any real value. Where are the deeper conceptual roots of such an approach? Many antique and medieval authors take the value of a product as independent from a given market situation; therefore, transporting it from one region/country where it is available in abundance to another region/country, where it is rare and highly sought after does not add any value in their perspective. In a similar vein, lending money at a certain time and taking it back later with interest does not seem to do so either. In fact, it was only the theory of marginal utility of the Modern economist Hermann Heinrich Gossen (1810–1858) to overcome this naturalistic fallacy.

In summary, the Aristotelian school's concept of the economy is in many ways bound to time and culture. First, it is addressing only male landowners, who belong to the class of decision-makers of the time. Relevant economic strategies could only be made by them – hence the philosopher explicitly addresses them and treats all other "stakeholders" as mere objects of his calculus. Moreover, *oikonomía* focused on agricultural production as the main driver of economic value creation in Greek society in the 4th century B.C. Other occupational groups – for example, traders, but also service providers of various kinds – were either overlooked or deliberately neglected. Furthermore, the book is characterized by a rather extended-family approach, which conceives the individual family, including its slaves, as the primary economic unit. This clearly reflects the specific climatic conditions and cultural traditions of ancient Greece. In contrast, riverine cultures such as ancient Egypt or China required more collective effort. Hence, they coordinated human labor during the flood phase and eventually developed much more collectivist institutions. In Europe, low population pressure and temperate climate allowed for greater economic autonomy and decentralized economic coordination. In doing so, the book describes the logic of a slave-holding culture, in which the privileges of the landowning class corresponded with the disenfranchised status of the exploited slaves and their families.

2.2 Economy in the Christian Holy Scriptures and Early Theological Documents

In an inter-religious comparison, it is striking, that the biblical scriptures themselves never explicitly mention the concept of Economy, economic wisdom, or related aspects. Hence, a contemporary New Testament manual does not contain the keyword *Economy*. The silence of the biblical scriptures in this regard marks a clear difference to the Holy scriptures of the other monotheist religions Judaism and Islam, which both contain explicit wisdom thought about different aspects of day-to-day life including Economic practices. There are multiple reasons for this striking fact. The most important factor is the eschatological horizon of the Jesus movement itself, which dominates the New Testament writings. As exegetical research has elaborated, the historical Jesus of Nazareth movement expected the end of history for the immediate future. Moreover, Jesus preached the dawning of the kingdom of God (*basileia tou theou*)[1], as already to be experienced in his own healing and liberating presence as well as in his original community. Especially at the beginning of his public preaching activity, he regarded his own signs and wonders as the catalyst bringing about the end of history. In this sense, the number of the twelve apostles represents a symbol of the twelve tribes of Israel as well as the twelve gates of the heavenly Jerusalem, the eschatological "new city". In Jesus' narratives about the heavenly Father, God is described as someone who radically overcomes the logic of the adequacy of performance and return that is so fundamental to good practice in economic scriptures. Consequently, Jesus himself refrained from reflections or exhortations on "good" economic practice. If he mentioned economics or economic elements at all in his sermons, it was as part of the "other", worldly hemisphere that would soon be overcome by the upcoming Basileia. For example, he exhorted his disciples to "render unto Caesar the things that are Caesar's, and unto God the things that are God's"[2] – thus clearly assigning money as the most important economic unit of measurement to the worldly sphere. Similarly, standing before Pontius Pilate, he explains: "My kingdom is not of this world. If my kingdom were of this world, my servants would have been fighting, that I might not be delivered over to the Jews. But as it is, my kingdom is not from the world"[3] . In this sense, it does not seem coincidental that – also according to the Gospel

---

[1] Mk 1:15
[2] Mt 22:15–22
[3] John 18:36

of John[4] – Judas as the disciple who eventually betrayed his Lord for the Price of thirty silver pieces[5], is reported as thieving treasurer of the community.

In contrast, during the Acts of the Apostles and the time of the first churches, collective ownership and unselfish sharing of worldly goods was supposed to represent the adequate Christian approach to Economy. This self-claim is also embodied in the early Christian communities combining religious practice with innovative economic behavior: living together in practiced communion of goods[6]. On the contrary, he or she who renounced to share or left the poor dying in their misery demonstrated a worldly character thereby risking his/her vocation to live in the kingdom of God. Thus, overcoming the worldly logic of 'Gift and gift in return' is defining the typical Christian. Because of this Eschatological character, a genuine discussion about Economic wisdom, which is contained in the Jewish bible or even in the Qur'an, is lacking in the early Christian scriptures.

The Apostle Paul emphasizes that there is no difference between slaves and freemen among Christians[7]. This becomes particularly clear in the letter to Philemon, whom he calls upon to accept his runaway and now baptized slave Onesimus as a beloved brother.[8] Here, for the first time in ancient writing, the personal dignity of the slave is expressed. On the other hand, Christianity does not contain a social revolutionary message – as it is shown in Paul's first letter to Timothy.[9] For the freedom that Jesus Christ gives is not dependent on external civil status.[10] In his letters, Paul leaves slavery itself – as a socially established form of ownership – untouched; however, he reminds slaves as well as masters of their mutual duties.[11] Following the lines of the Eschatological preaching of Jesus, however, Paul does not draw any consequences of the Christian anthropology for the design of a genuine Christian Economy.

For the upcoming decades, this silence about Economic structures was prolonged because of the fact that Early Christian communities were scattered among different cities and ethnic groups of the Ancient Roman Empire. In each place, they thereby represented mostly poor and uneducated members of

---

4 John 12:6.
5 Mt 26:15
6 Acts 4–5
7 Gal 3:28; Col 3:11; 1 Cor 12:13
8 Phm 15–17
9 1 Tim 6:1–2
10 1 Cor 7:22
11 Col 3:22–4:1; Eph 6:1–9

their local societies:[12] Christians therefore did not qualify for what Antique authors like Aristotle perceived as an appropriate audience for a treatise about Economy. Hence, both philosophical and socio-economic peculiarities conditioned the disturbed relationship of early Christianity towards Economy. Further on in history, the decay of the Roman Empire and the multiple instabilities and discontinuities resulting from it, reinforced the intellectual development of Christianity in the same direction. It is true that with the Constantinian Turn, the Christian religion lost its social marginality and gradually moved into a position of dominance as the Roman state religion. Consequently, Christian Church Fathers now represented influential public intellectuals; of course, they also developed sermons and instructions concerning Economic aspects. However, the political instability of the Roman empire fostered neo-platonic tendencies, which again emphasized finiteness and transience of the worldly existence.

As a prominent example, the theologian and philosopher Augustine of Hippo became of crucial importance not only for his own contemporaries; rather, he had also a deep impact on the Christian world view during the upcoming centuries. In his ample opus, Augustine elaborated about Human sin, church, and sacraments; but also about just war, coercion and faith, astrology, epistemology and ethics, sexuality, and pedagogy etc. In the context of our topic, his statements about slavery became of particular interest – given the fact that at this time slaves still represented a crucial pillar of the Economy.

In contrast to the Apostle Paul in his letter to Philemon, Augustine not only admonished Christians to accepts their slaves as brothers; rather he explicitly condemned slavery as a social institution. Consequentially, in his position as Bishop of Hippo in Northern Africa, he instructed his communities to free their slaves. Augustine highly appreciated Human intellect and rationality and therefore condemned slavery of Humans as an act of sin. Thereby, he even admonished the Roman Emperor to act against slaveholders which were buying and selling Human children. As a rational being, man should not reign over (other) rational beings but rather over animals. Thus, according to Augustine, slavery will be eradicated with the end of time. Until then, however, similarly to Paul he postulated a spiritual liberation – in the sense that a free slave should not serve his master in fear but in faithful love. Augustine's most influential book 'De Civitate Dei' demonstrates the strong influence, contemporary traditions of Neoplatonism (Plotin) and Stoicism exerted on him. Facing a manifest cultural crisis during his lifetime – with the Roman Empire gradually disappearing in the Migrational Period – he again oriented his hopes and reflections towards

---

12 1 Cor 1:26

the end of history; therefore, he again did not call for reforms to level up the social standards of his times. It is no coincidence that Augustine, as a convinced supporter of human rationality, was also one of the first in the intellectual history of Christianity to deal with natural law, which is closely related to the concept of human rationality.

2.2.1 Excurse: *Economia* as a Topic in Systematic Theology

During the history of Christian theology, Economy does not only stand for what we mainly understand by this term today. Rather, it also had a genuine theological meaning – also shaped, however, by the Greek origins mentioned above. What exactly is the context of this systematic-theological dimension and what did this term express? 'Economy' was used in contrast to 'theology' (in the original sense of 'word about God', Christian doctrine), here. In that respect, economy describes God's 'management'/'dealing' and 'stewardship' of the world – including salvation history, the birth, life and death of Jesus Christ, the early church, and the salvation ministry of the church. While in Christianity 'theology' is reserved for the (doctrinal) divine truths as such (e.g., the doctrine of the Divine Trinity of Father, Son, and Holy Spirit), in contrast the economy of salvation includes God's self-presentation/self-revelation in human history and the emergence of the Church. Thereby, *theology* as such remains a 'mysterium fidei', a miracle of faith, which to some extent even eludes rational comprehensibility and empirical derivability; while the divine *economy* can very well be traced and understood interpretatively by theologians and believers. Hence, it is only through *economy* that we know of *theology*. Or – as the Catholic Church's legal Code 'Codex Iuris Canonici' expresses: *Through the Economy, the Theology is revealed to us; but conversely, only the Theology illuminates the whole Economy. God's works reveals who He is in himself; the mystery of His being enlightens our understanding of his works – like a person discloses him-/ herself in her actions, and the better we know the person, the better we understand her actions.*[13]

In the context of the Christian bible, this terminology is used in the last scriptures of the canon, particularly by the Letter to the Ephesians[14] and in the First letter to Timothy.[15] Subsequently, it was originally employed in the writings of the Greek church fathers (i.e. much referred-to early theologians from the

---

13 § 236 CIC
14 Eph 1:10, 3:2, 3:9
15 1 Tim 1:4

2nd to the 7th century AD) and in the whole Byzantine tradition. Here, the Orthodox mystical tradition even claimed to possess *direct* access to divine truth (the *theology*) beyond taking the path of interpreting God's historical self-revelation (*economy*).

The mentioned mystical tradition in the church is formed by a long series of representatives. Early Christian mystics were Justin Martyr (1st century), Athanasius of Alexandria (3rd century), Augustine of Hippo (354–430), Pseudo-Dionysius the Areopagite (c. 500). Medieval and early modern mythicists include John Scotus Eriugena (c. 810 – c. 877), Bernard of Clairvaux (1090–1153), Hildegard of Bingen (1098–1179), Hugh of St Victor and Richard of St. Victor (12th century), Francis of Assisi (c.1182–1226), Anthony of Padua (1195–1231), Bonaventure (c. 1217–1274), Mechthild of Magdeburg (c. 1212 – c. 1297), Meister Eckhart (1260–1327), Johannes Tauler (14th century), Catherine of Siena (1347–1380), Teresa of Ávila (1515–1582), John of the Cross (Juan de Yepes) (1542–1591), Jakob Böhme (1575–1624), Angelus Silesius (1624–1677). Modern representatives of Christian mysticism also exist – such as Mary of the Divine Heart Droste zu Vischering (1863–1899), Andrew Murray (1828–1917), Frank Laubach (1884–1970), Padre Pio of Pietrecina (1887–1968), Thomas Merton (1915–1968), Adrienne von Speyr (1902–1967), Roger Schütz (1915–2005), Chiara Lubich (1920–2008) and others must be mentioned, here. For the role of all these people within the Christian tradition, the relationship of *economia* and *theologia* still plays a role: It represents a kind of 'grammar rule' for the acceptance of their message as a legitimate manifestation of Christian faith. On the protestant side, the equivalent for § 236 CIC mentioned above is the strong criticism of certain types of mysticism by M. Luther and Reformist theologians. They forcefully contested any mystical claim of a 'direct' access to God independent from the history of Salvation in Jesus Christ. Hence, the mutual referral of *theologia* and *economia* is commonly reaffirmed among the most important confessional groups of Christian tradition. More recently, the dualism between economy and theology became an important structural feature in the Oeuvre of the Catholic Theologian Hans-Urs von Balthasar (1905–1988), who – in the context of his monumental book 'Herrlichkeit' (Glory) – authored four books on 'Theo-Dramatik' (representing the Divine Economy) and three books on 'Theo-logik'.

Derived from the concept of Divine economy described above, subsequently the notion of 'ecclesiastical economy' emerged. In a similar vein, this described the 'handling'/ 'management' of diverse pastoral or disciplinary issues by Church representatives. For example, in the New Testament book Acts (of Apostels) 15th chapter, the early Christian leaders decide to repeal certain Jewish cultish commandments to be able to better integrate Gentile converts and non-Jewish newly baptized Christians in a better way. Here, the 'Economy according to leniency is differentiated from the 'Economy according to strictness/ preciseness' (Greek: *akribeia*). The former implied a certain 'handling' of the religious practice to facilitate the mission and salvation of certain groups. Later, dispensations inside of the Catholic Church law were legitimized in that perspective of 'ecclesiastical economy'.

2.3 Autonomy of Economic Affairs: Natural Law Tradition and Two Swords / Two Kingdoms Doctrines

As already mentioned, the Aristotelian school as well as Augustine's work on economy had a strong influence on what Medieval authors like Thomas Aquinas defined as 'natural law'. They took up the argument and continued it independently in the light of the Christian revelation. What resulted here, however, may be qualified as a 'conservative strain' of Christian Economics. In which sense?

The Aristotelian/ Augustine/ Thomistic work focus on 'natural law'. The latter – whether intentionally or not – brings about a general affirmation of the existing income inequalities, especially the property rights of the rich landowners. As a result, the unequal distribution of income in feudal agrarian society was moderated only by the moral exhortation to share abundance with the poor (like the late Roman Saint Martin of Tours had done at his time, sharing his soldier's coat with a beggar), by compassion with the sick and needy, by donations to the church etc. The differentiation between natural and supernational corresponds with Church father Augustine's (354–430) differentiation between the city of God and the secular earthly city.

We have already dealt with the Constantinian turn in the 4th century AD, which transformed Christianity into the mainstream religion of the outgoing Roman Empire. During the early Middle Ages, Christian rulers such as Charlemagne (748–814) reinforced that move. In this context, the Christian church became an important governing institution of the medieval feudal system – with the Roman pope as "spiritual leader" competing with the temporal power of emperors and kings. Moreover, in Germany the bishops rose to becoming independent feudal lords of their lands, also subject to appointment by the emperor. Some medieval popes spoke out strongly against slavery. Pope John VIII, for example, declared in the bull Unum est (873) that it could not be justified according to the teachings of Christ. In a similar vein, Pius II condemned the slave trade as a great crime, and condemned enslavement in a bull (1462). Contrarily, however, the political entanglement of the Church is mirrored also by diverging statements. Although Christians were no longer allowed to enslave their fellow believers, the papal bulls Dum diversas (1452) and Romanus Pontifex (1455) allowed them to enslave Muslim Saracens, pagans and other enemies of Christianity and take their property.

As far as the perception of Economy in Christianity is concerned, theological teachings reflect their ambivalent character. For example, in his bull 'Unam Sanctam' (1302), Pope Boniface III distinguishes between the two swords in this world: the spiritual sword of the church and the secular sword of the state. In this document, the Pope argues: Since the flesh is inferior to the soul,[16] the (temporal) sword of the state is of lesser dignity; nevertheless, even if the church is superior to the state, the autonomy of the secular sphere must be acknowledged. 'Unam sanctam', a very influential document of the medieval theological discussion, reflects the political power struggle between popes and emperors during the Middle Ages. At the same time, however, it also brings about important consequences for the development of 'economy' in Christianity. This is because the distinction and separation of the two swords as such effectively shielded the socio-economic order of the Feudal economic order against emancipative social-ethical critique and innovation from the spiritual sphere. Thus, the "two swords" doctrine – together with the natural law traditions – helped to reaffirm the enormous social inequalities the feudal order brought to medieval society. It effectively separated the realm of Economy from the (potentially) emancipative dynamic of Christian Spirituality.

The Reformation – continuing and complementing the efforts of earlier unsuccessful protest reform initiatives – sharply criticized the worldly power structure of the Catholic Church and invoked the freedom of (individual) Christian persons. In general, however, the reformatory process was limited to confessional emancipation, new liturgical practices, and church organization. On the contrary, no attention was paid to a comparable critique of economic inequalities or to initiating corresponding reforms. Rather, the emerging Lutheran-Protestant churches were again dominated by the new type of political leaders, the dukes, landlords, sovereigns, etc. Consequently, the protestant clergy also became an important part of the social hierarchy in their territories. Martin Luther's "two kingdoms/two regimes doctrine" – which was also accepted by some reformist theologians – emphasized that God exercises his power through two kingdoms: the kingdom of law/old Adam and the kingdom of grace. As people of faith, Christians live in both kingdoms/realities. Therefore, driven by faith in God's grace, they may personally choose to donate or share their wealth with the poor. This did not imply, however, that they supported economic or political initiatives/projects to improve the lot of the disenfranchised; nor did they launch

---

16 Mt 10:28

corresponding 'emancipatory' pro-poor socio-economic initiatives in the medieval/early modern economy. Consequently, conceptual dualism in theology – reemphasized in the work of Martin Luther – in turn led to a continuation of the mainstream conservative orientation in Lutheran socio-ethical positions, which effectively legitimized the status quo of an extremely unjust feudal society.

These reactionary tendencies also appeared in Luther's position against the farmer's protests in 1524–1526. Inspired by his writings about the Christian freedoms, poor and exploited farmers mostly in south-western parts of the Holy Roman Empire revolted against their landlords as well as the local clerical elite. Thomas Müntzer, a protestant theologian and personal confidant of Luther during his stay at Wittenberg, sympathized with the postulates of the farmers and with the twelve programmatic articles they had formulated. From today's point of view, these Articles represent an impressive document in Christian religious tradition incriminating exploitative economic practices and calling for the economic rights of an incriminated social group. Moreover, the twelve articles are regarded as the first public record of human rights/ freedoms in Europe; the farmer group assembly they emerged from appears as the first constituent assembly in Germany. Here, the insurgents set themselves uniform goals, ranging from the mere restoration of their customary rights (which had been progressively curtailed by the landlords) to the abolition of serfdom and claiming basic democratic rights in a representative assembly. Moreover, as Luther in his writings had successfully invoked the scriptural principle ('sola scriptura'), they also proclaimed their divine right to argue autonomously in the light of written documents. Like him, they declared themselves ready to drop their demands as soon as they were proven wrong from the Bible. This reference to Luther, a nationally known Reformation theologian and publicist, was intended to help their cause achieve a breakthrough and strengthen their hopes for social liberation. However, the hope of being supported by the leading intellectual were bitterly disappointed. It is true that in the pamphlet "Exhortation to Peace on the Twelve Articles of the Peasantry in Swabia" he had initially expressed some understanding for the postulates of the peasants and had qualified their twelve articles as partially legitimate; moreover, he had critically addressed both sides, princes, and peasants, and called the princes to end exploitative practices. In May 1525, however, threatened by the violent activities of the insurgent peasants, Luther rather appealed to the secular authorities to fight them mercilessly. In a famous sentence he demanded that the rebels should be 'crushed, strangled and stabbed like a rabid dog', because otherwise the country would perish.

What was the background of the furor, which spoke out of these words of the great Reformer? On a trip to his native town Eisleben, Luther had just preached on the Christian's willingness to suffer. In response, however, his auditorium grew angry, rejected the Reformer's claim, and repeated Thomas Müntzer's doctrine of the equality of all Human beings before God. Immediately after this disturbing experience, and because the insurgent farmers were killing a princely administrator on Eastern 1525, Luther quickly authored his writing ‚Against the Murderous and Robber Rotten of the Peasants'. Here, he condemned the uprisings as the work of the devil and called upon all princes of whatever denomination to put down the peasants with all necessary force. Thereby, he denounced Müntzer as the arch-devil of Mühlhausen. When the rebellion found its end with the battle of Frankenhausen in 1526, Müntzer was captured and beheaded, his head impaled on a stake. More than 6000 farmers were slaughtered by the armed forces of the local princes.

This episode of bloody confrontation between Luther and Müntzer again demonstrates the conservative character of the dominant Christian interpretations of Economy. Dualistic concepts strictly separated the spiritual from reforming the 'worldly' sphere. Rather, the later – with the Economy being an important part of it – was supposed to be regulated by 'natural law'. Hence, it remained effectively shielded against any 'utopian' or emancipative spiritual impulse. On the other hand, social idealists like Müntzer fell prey to their abstract spiritual criticism and drowned in a maelstrom of confrontation and violence. Thereby, they systematically ignored the role of economic wisdom for attaining social prosperity and the emergence of humanitarian standards. Reducing the challenge of a value-based "Christian economy" to the overthrow of existing power relations, social revolutions prepared the ground for violent atrocities and ultimately contributed to a reaffirmation of the conservative mainstream: a mistake that was to prove even more disastrous as history progressed.

2.4 The Monastic Tradition and the Emergence of Christian Economy Practices

Already in late antiquity (Benedict of Nursia 525) and especially during the Middle Ages, monasteries and monastic theological communities were constituted as a counterweight to the power structure of the Christian Church. Here, communities of men or women lived together to pray, work and study and subsequently formed educational and cultural centers of a growing medieval society. In the context of a family-based social order, the monastic way of life and the cooperatively self-organizing communities themselves represented an important social innovation. Subsequently, they increasingly became intellectual centers and lighthouses of Christian orientation in their regions. Moreover, monasteries and monastic theologians gave rise to a variety of impulses for innovative social practices. In contrast to the abstract dualism described above – tearing apart spiritual enthusiasm on the one hand and conservative reaffirmation of social power structures on the other – monastic communities like the Benedictine, Franciscan, Dominican societies developed elements of 'emancipative' social practices internally and externally. For example, the 'regula Benedicti' over centuries brought about alternative forms of Governance, in which Christian values translate into concrete rules of organizing a community: for example, elements of an egalitarian community, in which younger and elder, more and less educated members, members with a richer or a poorer social background lived together and developed a culture of discussion and cooperation. As recent economic research has shown, the 'Regula Benedicti' are full of Economic wisdom and knowledge of 'good governance', which contributed to the extraordinary organizational longevity of the Benedictine monasteries, lasting more than 500 years on average[17]. Hildegard of Bingen in her sisters-community developed a tangible spirituality – with consequences for the health situation of poorer people, for an every-day spirituality etc. with very tangible economic consequences. In addition, monastic and lay communities brought about a variety of social, economic, and technical innovations: for example, the double-entry book-keeping of the Franciscan monk Luca Pacioli (1445 – 1517), which became a cornerstone of modern business practices. European architecture received significant impulses from the Cistercian Order, which no longer wanted to be financed by dependent farmers but by its own work. The Cistercian work ethics of precision, order and continuity – brought about by other monastic communities as well – represented frontrunners for the modern business culture.

It is also true that monasteries during the centuries often grew rich because of donations of bequests and their own diligent work culture. Hence, monasteries became power structures themselves – with many of them not hesitating even to own slaves and to exploit villeins. At the same time, however, monasteries as educational centers also started important social reform initiatives. In this sense, Harold J. Berman[18] pointed towards monastic judges at church courts, which were influencing the emerging Western legal tradition during the early Middle Ages. Here, monastic administrators and judges represented a kind of 'left-wing-intellectuals' of medieval times; on the one hand they were well-educated, on the other hand, they had no personal 'vested interests' like educated rich

---

[17] Inauen, Emil / Frey, Bruno S. / Rost, Katja / Osterloh, Margit, "Benedictine Tradition and Good Governance," in: Luigino Bruni / Barbara Sena (eds.), *The Charismatic Principle in Social Life*, Routledge Frontiers of Political Economy, 2012.

[18] Berman, Richard, *Law and Revolution. The Formation of the Western Legal Tradition*, Cambridge: Harvard University Press, 1983.

landholders, who strove to increase the wealth of their heritage. Consequently, within the framework of Medieval judicial practice the monk-judges repeatedly pressed for contractual arrangements and worked against the feudal landowners' demand for feudal manual and tensile services. Over the decades, this tendency substantially contributed to push back feudalist exploitation and to reinforce voluntary contract agreements as basis of exchange in the economy. As a result, the economic freedom and autonomy of poorer persons were strengthened. The judicial practice of the monastic judges represented an early manifestation of what was to find expression centuries later as the principle of personhood in Christian social ethics and social reform initiatives.

Barnabas of Terni belonged to a noble family of the Umbrian region and was a well-educated man, Doctor of Medicine with good knowledge of contemporary letters and philosophy as well. In his early years, Barnabas entered the Franciscan Order in the Umbria province of the order and became a monk. A gifted preacher full of spirituality, he was entrusted with many tasks by his confreres. Barnabas was very concerned about the problem of poor families lacking access to savings or credit opportunities. Due to the church law forbidding usury and any lending of money for payment of interest, poor people in need were obliged to consult the money lender – during that time mostly Jewish people, to which it was forbidden to execute any farming or production work. Other lending groups were the Lombards, a kind of travelling bankers, whose interest rates were often even higher, usually being $43\frac{1}{2}$ per cent, and frequently as high as 80 per cent.

In the medieval Italian cities, Montes (Latin word for 'mountains', from the "heaped together" deposits) had been founded some years before: banks that paid out interest in exchange for a deposit of money. On the one hand, Montes served to finance the municipality; on the other, they provided regular income to persons with small fortunes. The first Montes institution emerged around 1300 in Florence and spread to other Italian cities. Picking up on the idea of the Montes but transforming it to work in favor of poor lending families, a Franciscan group around Barnabas in 1462 founded the first Monte di Pietà at Perugia, giving the go-ahead for quite a few followers in various Italian cities: in Orvieto in 1463, in Viterbo in 1471, in Bologna in 1473, in Savona in 1479, in Milan in 1483, in Mantova, Assisi, Brescia and Ferrara in 1484, in Vicenza in 1486, in Forlì in 1510, in Naples in 1539. All these institutions remained independent of each other under the auspices of the respective municipality, they lended money to their own needy inhabitants. The financial capital of a Monte di Pietà was raised by the founders – mostly Franciscan monks – through endowments and collections, many of them from Jewish lenders themselves. Moreover, rich people could also deposit their wealth within the Mons Pietatis – thereby temporarily freeing themselves from the Christian duty to donate or from the need to protect their wealth against theft. Within the Mons Pietatis credit was granted to poor people against pledges such as jewelry, clothing or appliances and was subject to interest. For the internal structure of the Mons, a director called depositarius was hired, an appraiser, a notarius or accountant, salesmen and other employees. Salaries were paid either with a fixed sum or with a percentage of the profits of the institution.

Hence, over time, fewer and fewer Montes Pietatis issued their loans interest-free; rather interests rates ranged from 4 to 12 percent. Subsequently, it was precisely this interest payment, which met the resistance of other theologians, who perceived it as usury and violation of the prohibition of interest. Critics did not admit that the use of the interest to maintain the charity justified the usury; rather they stated, that a good end could not justify evil means. Here, it was held that lending money at interest was intrinsically bad, money being unfruitful by its nature. As a reaction, in some places 'montes gratuiti' were founded, especially in Lombardy, which abandoned interest payment. However, since these charities could not sustain themselves, they were subsequently returned into institutions with interest. Moreover, theologians such as Bernardino da Feltre argued for defense of the regular mons with the need for interest payments to ensure the permanence of the institution. At the end of each month or of each year, the net profits were added to the capital, and if they were considerable, the interest rate was reduced. To increase the funds of the Mons Pietatis, collections were regularly held in some cities on certain days – in Padua on Easter Day – or boxes were placed for donations, as in Gubbio and Orvieto. In Gubbio, a small tax was levied on all property bequeathed by will, and in Spello the notary had to remind the testator to leave something to the monastery (Catholic Encyclopedia). Initially, the sums handed out in the Mons Pietatis were rather small. This served the goal to avoid speculation or extravagance. With more and more organizations spreading across Italy, however, the amount was gradually raised – in some places up to 100 and even to 1000 ducats. In general, the amount of a loan corresponded to approximately two-thirds of the value of the object pledged, which, if not redeemed within the established lending period, was sold at a public auction, and if the price obtained was higher than the loan plus interest, the surplus was paid to the owner (Catholic Encyclopedia).

Summing-up, the "Montes Pietatis" represented an important social innovation of the medieval economy: early forms of charitable and cooperative banking, which can be perceived even as forerunners of today's microfinance organizations. Even if some Montes Pietatis suffered bankruptcy – often due to mismanagement or fraught, they represent an important step for a qualified concept of Economy in Christianity. As an expression of Franciscan spirituality, these organizations granted loans to the poor and disadvantaged against payment of interest. During the 19th century, the Montes developed into savings and associative banks, thereby playing an important role in the economic development of rural areas in many parts of (mostly: Western and Southern) Europe.

Beyond these developments, however, the emergence of the Montes Pietatis represents a crucial paradigm shift in the history of the Christian concept of Economy. As seen above, Christian authors during the antique and medieval times had mostly accepted the economic status quo of their Economies, which were based on the exploitation of slaves and later of feudal dependencies. In a similar vein, even Paul's letter to Philemon had basically accepted slavery as an institution of the worldly order and had limited itself to a recommendation to the slaveholder for treating the returning slave Onesimus well. Christian authors before the Franciscan monks perceived the general Economic situation as an expression of 'natural law' or attributed it to the 'fallen' character of the worldly existence. Despite enormous injustices and the outrageous poverty, in which large parts of the populace had to strive for making a living, they thereby limited Christian 'modifications' to the personal realm of pious mercy.

With the Franciscan spirituality of the late medieval times, this approach changed for the first time. A Christian perception of Economy did not remain exclusively oriented towards the hereafter, while the existing institutions were accepted as a necessary given. Rather, Christian values claim validity in relation to the socio-economic structures of the world. In the context of the Franciscan movement of the late medieval period (Nominalism etc.), Christian orientation should also impact contemporary society and translate into an institutionally effective, emancipative reform impulses[19] – even if their transformation into an explicit Social Ethical approach would take another 350 years.

2.5 Overcoming 'Natural Law': The Emergence of Economics as an Academic Subject

During the 18th century, the modern concept of Economics gradually evolved as a secular research discipline dealing with the production, distribution, and trade, as well as consumption of goods and services by different agents. This happened in a typical Enlightenment perspective, in which the world was perceived as a regulated universe. God represented the creator of the universe, who determined

---

[19] Schallenberg, Peter, "Die franziskanische Spiritualität und eine christliche Moralökonomik (Einführung zur deutschen Ausgabe)," in: Luigino Bruni / Stefano Zamagni (eds.), *Zivilökonomie, Effizienz, Gerechtigkeit, Gemeinwohl* (Christliche Sozialethik im Diskurs 1), Paderborn 2013, 13–29.

'natural laws' and subsequently refrained from continuously intervening. Rather, he had left the universe as a clockwork ticking according to its own rules. In this sense, the Scottish moral philosopher Adam Smith (1723–1790) – generally referred to as father of modern Economics – when teaching at the University of Glasgow (1751–1764) held a Chair for 'Moral philosophy/ Theologia naturalis'. This implied that he was supposed to teach the socio-economic laws of the Divine order, according to which commerce and economic exchange must be organized. Hence, Economics as an academic discipline, on the background of the prevailing cosmology of the early modern times/ Age of Enlightenment, started as a 'Christian' discipline. Like the Natural Sciences, whose success in formulating 'laws of nature' impressed the intellectuals of these times, Economics should inquire the 'laws of economy', of economic activities, national differences, exchange and trade – to be recognized by politicians and authorities as well as practitioners in a general way.

Pretty much in line with these expectations, Adam Smith (who was a practicing member of the Protestant Church of Scottland) elaborated on the anthropological foundations of Moral Decision making ("Theory of Moral Sentiments', 1759) as well as on the reasons for income differences between different regions and countries ('An Inquiry into the Nature and Causes of the Wealth of Nations', 1776). Thus, his main (liberal) thesis about the self-regulation of economic markets (figuratively expressed by the motif of the 'invisible hand') represented a pledge for non-intervention of the Government into the market clearing process – in a similar way as God had also renounced to intervene in the regulation of the natural cosmos.

On the other hand, Smith certainly did not argue against any form of moral argument regarding economic processes and their outcome. Rather Smith is generally perceived as a 'Scottish moral philosopher' (together with David Hume, Francis Hutcheson and others), a group of theorists, who explicitly claimed to instruct moral reasoning by – among others – emphasizing the systemic interdependencies of modern social practice. For that purpose, they showed that some political interventions may effectively bring about counterintuitive and negative consequences, if they do not reflect on 'economic laws'.

In the perspective of our topic, the concept of Economy in Christianity, the emergence of economics as an academic subject dealing with Human economic behavior and national Economies in general brought about a double step: First, it outlines the challenge of realizing (Christian) values in the economic reality. Hence, the traditional Western dualism between Eschatology and mundane reality is transferred into a duality of normative (=ethical) and positive (= functional) level of analysis. Realizing a 'good' Economy – in the sense of transforming religiously founded values into Economic practice – does no longer seem impossible, because values and practice would belong to different ontological spheres. Rather, social innovations and reform initiatives seem possible if they follow the 'laws' of the Economy.

By extending scientific analysis from natural science to the social and economic sphere, economic authors during the 19th and 20th century gradually overcame a 'natural law' perspective, which had stabilized economic inequality and a poverty trap for large parts of the population for centuries. Rather it became clear that in the context of an Industrialized society, with adequate social policies, ethical goals could be realized to a much larger extent than expected before. Hence, social reform and social policy became an issue for religious believers, who strove to transform Christian values of Human rights and social justice into practice.

Second, the work of Adam Smith and other Scottish moral philosophers like David Hume or Bernhard Mandeville differentiated between the level of the individual (micro-) Economy (tackled also by the works of Aristotle or Thomas) and the national (macro) Economy taken care of by the Government or by the political authorities in general. While moral sentiments or altruism does indeed play a role for the micro-economy (and for many religion-based value systems), it does not seem relevant as a control variable for the macro-economy. Hence, economic theory makes clear that the national economy cannot just be conceptualized in the same logic as an individual household; rather it must be analyzed and understood in its own logic.

To proceed in that endeavor, many academic Economists of the post-classical period had originally been trained as Natural scientist, mathematicians, Physicists etc. For example, during the first half of the 19th century, the philosopher Auguste Comte (influenced by the work of the physician Isaac Newton) had developed a vision of 'social physics'. Subsequently, during the industrial age of the late 19th century, the equilibrium theories of Alfred Marshall, Vilfredo Pareto and Francis Edgeworth were based on the work of mathematicians like James Clerk Maxwell or Ludwig Boltzmann, who had done work on the statistical behavior of individual agents. According to the prevailing academic attitudes derived from Natural Sciences, a body of economic knowledge was created in a rather abstract academic process. For that purpose, reference was made to abstract cumulative notions like states of equilibrium (for example between supply and demand in a certain market), their dynamic adaptation processes, stationary states of different markets (for employment, money, credit etc.) etc. As a result of these scientific developments, analytical research about the Economy often lost sight of a normative dimension. Moreover, the role of Human actors and of (social) Innovation as a driving force for social change and for a better life was hidden behind mathematical formulas. In this situation, it was Harvard-Professor

Joseph Schumpeter's work to emphasize Entrepreneurship as '*creative destruction*' and understand it as an indispensable characteristic of capitalist Economies. This concept, published in Schumpeter's path breaking book 'Capitalism, Socialism and Democracy' (1942) became a cornerstone for the contemporary discussion about Entrepreneurship and Social Innovation. It inspired authors like Acemoglu & Robinson[20], Clayton Christensen[21], Philipp Aghion[22] and others. Even religious roots of these perspectives become obvious. Recently, the roots of the concept of creative destruction in early Egyptian mythology (Phoenix), in the Hindu Goddess Shiva as dancing destroyer, in the works of Goethe, Marx, Nietzsche and Sombart was made transparent[23]. However, also for an innovation-centered approach towards the Economy, deep roots in the Jewish-Christian traditions are also obvious. Especially, innovation as the center of a modern economy was described as a process of constant disruption and change. This shows manifold references to narratives and motives from the Jewish-Christian traditions, where openness to change and innovation finds its narrative expression right from the beginning. One famous example is the Patriarch Abraham, whom all three monotheistic world religions (Judaism, Christianity and Islam) recognize as their "father in faith". Aged 75, he still leaves the traditional social order of his home city of Haran.[24] This was done in faith in God's unspecified promise of a land in which his descendants would be numerous, and he would be a blessing to all peoples. In a similar way, the early Christian tradition is also characterized by the expectation of an eschatological change and a (radical) innovation, as seen above.

---

20 Acemoglu, Darin / Robinson, James, *Why Nations Fail. The Origins of Power, Prosperity, and Poverty*, New York: Crown Business, 2012.
21 Christensen, Clayton M., *The Innovator's Dilemma: When new technologies cause great firms to fail*, Boston, Massachusetts, USA: Harvard Business School Press, 1997.
22 Aghion, P. /Antonin, C. / Bunel, S., *The Power of Creative Destruction. Economic Umheaval and the Wealth of Nations*, Cambridge MA: The Belknap Press of Harvard University Press, 2021.
23 Reinert, Hugo / Reinert, Erik S., "Creative Destruction in Economics: Nietzsche, Sombart, Schumpeter," in: J. Backhaus / W. Drechsler (eds.), *Friedrich Nietzsche (1844–1900)*, Boston: Springer, 2006, 55–85.
24 Gen 11 ff.

2.6 The Emergence of Christian Social Ethics during the Industrialization

During the 19th and 20th century, Industrialization and modernization brought about a radical transition of the living conditions not only for small elite minorities, but also for uneducated workers. A high number of young and poorly trained rural dwellers – many of them Catholic – flowed into the modern cities and ended up as simple laborers under precarious economic, social, and spiritual situations. They found themselves exposed to what we would call today a completely uncivilized capitalism and market economy. Lacking access to basic labor and social institutions, financial insecurity, and the inability to feel at home at this new urban environment characterizes their situation[25].

This challenging transition process fueled skepticism among Christian intellectuals, clerics and theologians about the whole project of industrialization. As a result, Christian philosophers, preachers, and public intellectuals stood in principled opposition to the emerging system of free-market enterprises and industrialized production. In a period of massive urbanization, for many of them Christian values seem indissolubly tied to the highly integrated village or small town ('Social Romanticism'). An opposite reaction to the transition described above was secular – and often economically based – criticism of religion, which propagated new values for a new World. Leading intellectuals like Karl Marx, Friedrich Engels, Ludwig Feuerbach, and others called for a Humanist and scientific critique of the religious tradition as well as for new secular and emancipatory values.

What we perceive, here, is a typically contemporary intellectual constellation of a counter-positioning between Christian Humanism on the one hand and (atheist) Economic Humanism on the other. With the rise of the Industrial age, a rather secular economic analysis emerged, which remains increasingly detached from its Christian anthropological roots. Subsequently, it gave birth to a materialist philosophical position represented by authors like Karl Marx and Friedrich Engels. For these authors, who were inspired by a historical-philosophical position of Hegel and others, Christianity – and more generally religion as whole – represents an instrument to legitimize exploitation of poor peasants and laborers by the landowners and capitalistic owner of the means of production. In such a perspective, which strives to promote a revolutionary turn-over of

---

25 Goldschmidt, N. / Habisch, A., "Western Religion, Social Ethics and Public Economics," in: F. Forte / R. Mudambi / P. Navarra (eds.), *A Handbook of Alternative Theories of Public Economics*, Cheltenham: Elgar, 2014, 198–226.

the existing Capitalist tenure, Christian hope for a heavenly afterlife is just illusionistic and distracting the working class from the necessary fight against exploitation. On the other extreme of the intellectual spectrum, Conservative Christian movements emerged, making front against materialism and consumerism, against sexual libertinage in the cities, against the decay of family values etc. Those groups fought their cultural wars against a modern economy. They condemned the pursuit of wealth redistribution and social reform as signs of decadent materialism and apostasy from the belief in paradise. In their perspective, it was not a 'change of conditions' – social reforms ('Bedingungswandel') – but a change of attitudes – in the sense of a revival of Christian spirituality ('Gesinnungswandel') – that would be required.

In this counter position of two opposing intellectual currents – economic criticism of Christian religion and Christian criticism of a modern economy – Christian Social Ethics emerged. It held fast to the Christian values tradition and accepted its validity, even if the whole structure of society had obviously undergone groundbreaking changes. At the same time, however, representatives did not limit themselves to religious practice but inspired by Christian values tried to positively influence the living conditions of the emerging industrial worker's class. Hence, in line with a modern concept of contingency awareness, they did not wait for the realization of Christian values in the heavenly beyond, but strove to develop new schemes for social ethical reflection beyond the traditional morality, etc. They overcame a scheme of moral duties/ transgressions but developed ethical principles like 'Solidarity', 'Subsidiarity' and 'Personality' to grant ethical orientation for action in the context of a diverse plurality of concepts. This new type of ethical principles did not limit the acting faithful person to a mere obedience to prefixed codes of behaviors; rather, they require the capability to exert personal responsibility, autonomously judge situations and adapt the principles accordingly.

A very prominent body of documents promoting Christian Social Teaching represent the Social Encyclicals of the Roman Pontiff, in which the Catholic church formulated normative perspectives for a Christian concept of Economy. For example, the first document of that kind, the Encyclical 'Rerum Novarum' of Pope Leo XIII. issued in 1891, during the quick growth of industrial production in Europe and North America, opposed the Marxist view that capitalism could be reduced to a mere exploitation of the worker's class by the capitalists and that workers should strive for social revolution. Rather the document pledged for the legitimacy of private property and the importance of family values even in the context of the industrial age. Pope Leo emphasized the personal value of workers and decried the social neglect by the dominant liberal policies of these years. 40 years later, the document 'Quadragesimo Anno' was co-authored by the German Jesuit theologian Oswald von Nell-Breuning (1931). It promoted the ideal of 'Subsidiarity', which emphasizes the power of self-organization structures in the context of a professional order. Here, Christian Social Thought opposed the dirigisme of the totalitarian dictatorships of fascist and communist regimes of the 1930ies – which ultimately brought about the total disaster of World War II and the decade-long agony of the Socialist economies in Eastern Europe. During the 1960/70s John XXIII. and Paul VI. called for a Global responsibility of political leaders and a common orientation towards Global Peace and Justice. Pope John Paul II. pledged for an economic order, which should be oriented towards the Personal dignity of Human workers (Laborem Exercens, Sollicitudo Rei Socialis); years later, after the breakdown of the socialist economies, John Paul II. elaborated the social role and responsibility of private Entrepreneurs (Centesimus Annus, 1991). Pope Benedict in his Encyclical 'Caritas in Veritate' emphasized the personal responsibility of Human persons as costumers and of the social responsibility of organizations/ companies. More recently, Pope Francis formulated the importance of the Environmental challenge for a reorientation of Global Business[26] etc.

Even if the Papal Encyclicals and other Church documents from catholic and protestant traditions remained the most publicly visible manifestations, the Christian Social Ethics was mostly driven by lay-people such as inspired leaders in (family-) businesses, media, academia. They adjusted their day-to-day decisions towards their Christian values – based on a concept of Human beings as endowed with Human dignity and organizations/ structures to be oriented towards solidarity in subsidiarity.

2.7 Particular Relevance of Christian Social Ethics for Germany

Following the principles mentioned above, socially engaged Christians overcame the limitations of personal piety or misery with the poor; rather they promoted the drafting of social institutions and rules of the Economic and Social System. In Germany, the most important intellectual protagonists of Christian Social Ethics – for example Jesuit fathers like H. Pesch, G. Gundlach, O. Nell-Breuning etc. – had started a second academic study in Economics after their theological exams. They strove to better understand the foundations of economics in order to propose social and economic change by institutional reform. Thereby,

---

26 *Laudato Si*, 2015

they directly or indirectly influenced Catholic politicians in the Christian oriented parties of the Weimar Republic – and subsequently in the Christian Democratic as well as the Social democratic party of the young Federal republic. Due to the genuine historical circumstances of two lost World Wars and the constant threat of totalitarian ideologies, Christian politicians happened to play a particularly important role in Germany. In fact, starting after the first World War, many institutions of the German social and labor system were implemented and remodeled by politicians and administrators inspired by a Christian mindset.

For example, in 1920 the first Minister for Labor and Social affairs of the democratic Weimar Republic Government became a man named Heinrich Brauns. Brauns happened to be a Catholic clergyman and had worked as a workers' priest, an activist in a Catholic Social Ethics NPO and later as a 'Centre party' leader. Subsequently from 1920–1928, Brauns modelled the labor system of the young Weimar republic. For example, he drafted the codetermination laws implementing Workers' councils (as institutionalized representatives of labor interests) in German companies; he implemented a (basic) public unemployment insurance system and a three-level system of labor courts, in which labor conflicts could be settled in a professional way; he founded the national network of employment agencies in every city – with the center organization located in Nuremberg, what became the Federal Employment Agency today.

After 1933, the totalitarian Nazi dictatorship overruled these institutions by drafting authoritarian structures. However, during the 1950ies and 60ies, the Federal Republic of Germany returned to the development path Brauns had opened and even completed it. Politicians of the Christian democratic party dominating the first Governments during these decades implemented a social security system, which was modelled according the principles of Solidarity and Subsidiarity – with priority given to the smaller decision units (communal bodies) while central authorities should only supervise and support. Accordingly, a network of regional social advocacy and labor organizations was created all over the country to fight poverty, qualify unemployed workers for a new job, grant unemployment insurance or social assistance for poor families etc.

After some years of economic development, access to public Schools and universities was granted free of charge, which enabled social uplifting of children from poor or disadvantaged families. During these formative years after the total disaster of World War II, Christian Social Ethics influenced the crafting of social and economic institutions not only in Germany, but in many other European countries like the Netherlands, Belgium and France as well ('Rhinish capitalism'). As a result, compared with two millennia of European history, we witness a completely new approach towards economy in Christianity. With advanced industrialization, the per capita surplus of economic growth and development exploded – thereby providing the financial basis for redistribution and the provision of public goods like education, infrastructure, professional legal and administrative systems etc. A national network of tax offices fueled the emergence of the Welfare state, as the fluidity and changeability of social institutions became also obvious. As a result, the status quo of social inequality was no longer taken as granted as it has been the case in medieval or modern times; rather social systems emerged, which should help to overcome discrimination, poverty, illiteracy, social isolation etc.

However, beyond mere Government/ policy-centered instruments, also the role of civil society, social innovators and social Entrepreneurs must be emphasized. Christian Union activists – for example of Coal miner's and steelworker's unions – played an important role in that process right from the beginning. A wide range of Christian press organs and associational publications emerged in the context of the Christian social movement – in order to support the emancipative engagement of Christian associations and labor activists/worker's priests on the ground. Moreover, a network of national Christian academies emerged for worker's education – comparable to the popular education movement of the social democrats.

Furthermore, right from the beginning, also Christian businessmen had played an important mediating role for the emergence of Christian Social Ethics. As cultural brokers, they bridged the chasm between the century-old Christian values tradition on the one hand and the pressing social and economic challenges of the emerging Industrial society on the other[27]. In the example of Germany, it was the Catholic textile Entrepreneur Franz Brandts, who co-founded a national NPO of crucial importance for recruiting and supporting Christian politicians like the above mentioned first minister for labor and social affairs, Heinrich Brauns. In 1914, the 'people's League for Catholic Germany' assembled already more than 1 Mio. members nation-wide. This organization represented a crucial mediator for sensitizing Christian practitioners – laymen as well as priests – for the challenges, Industrialization had brought about for Catholic worker families. It produced a rich literature – with a special focus on Economic contents – for

---

27 Habisch, André / Loza Adaui, Cristian R., "The Charisma of a Conservative Innovator: Franz Brandts and the Rise of the "Christlich-soziale Bewegung" in Germany in the Age of Industrialization," in: L. Bruni / B. Sena (eds.): *The Charismatic Principle in Economic and Civil Life: History, Theory and Good Practice*, Florence, n.p. 2011. Habisch, André, "Practical Wisdom for Social Innovation: How Christian Entrepreneurs Triggered the Emergence of the Catholic Social Tradition in Europe," in: J.G. Backhaus / G. Chaloupek / H.A. Frambach (eds.), *On the Economic Significance of the Catholic Social Doctrine. 125 years of Rerum Novarum*, Cham, Switzerland: Springer, 2017, 167–190.

instructing emerging Christian Labour-Unions and Social solidarity groups and help them assert their emancipative concerns in a more effective way. Because of the activities of Brauns and other Christian politicians, the 'people's League' – albeit mostly forgotten today – played an important role for the Social market economy in post WW II Germany.

Another example is Leon Harmèl, a French textile Entrepreneur and contemporary of Brandts on the other side of the French-German border. Harmèl was very committed for textile workers and organized several pilgrimages to Rome. Playing an important role as a volunteer official in the Vatican as well, he became crucial for 'Rerum Novarum', the first Social Encyclical starting the corresponding tradition. Concerning the role of business leaders for realizing Christian values in the economy, UNIAPAC, the gobal network of Catholic Entrepreneurship Associations worldwide, has recently published a paper 'The vocation of the Business Leader: A reflection', which carefully elaborates the different aspects of Christian business leadership in a global perspective.[28]

Much more would have to be added in that respect, which cannot be done in the context of this survey article. Generally speaking, however, it remains clear: If many European Economies today are still dominated by socio-economic practices orientated towards an equilibrium of Innovation *and* social partnership, this is also due to the long-term consequences of social, economic and political commitment inspired by the Jewish-Christian value tradition.

3 Summing-up: Economy in Christianity

As our historical tour de raison makes clear, Economy (and Economics) was never a familiar housemate in Christianity. The history of the term begins centuries before Jesus Christ; if it played any role in the early Christian documents at all, then as an element of the worldly age, which is supposed to come to an end with the immediately expected 'Kingdom of God'. Christians are to live in this world, but not to be ruled by its (economic) laws.

As the attitude towards slavery impressively illustrates, this dualistic logic prevailed – for different reasons – during the first centuries of the history of Christianity. After the Apostles' Summit in the year 30 AD, Christianity developed as a polyethnic religion – with very few rich and powerful believers in the rows of their scattered communities. Thus, a genuine Economic wisdom tradition – comparable to what we find in the holy scriptures of Judaism or Islam – does

---

[28] https://uniapac.org/wp-content/uploads/2019/11/The-Vocation-of-Business-Leader-ENG.pdf.

not find itself developed in the Christian New Testament. Consequently, due to the important role of Ancient Greek and Roman cultural traditions in the theological teachings of the Medieval church, the dualism prevailed. At the same time, however, medieval monasteries played an important role for overcoming the chasm between Eschatological expectations and socio-economic quietism in the face of the enormous social differences of the antique and medieval societies. With the emergence of modern economics, the knowledge of the malleability and formability of the National economy and society started to grow substantially. With the dawning of the Industrial Age, first documents of an explicit 'Christian Social Thought' emerged – setting orientation marks for an Economy inspired by the Christian values tradition. Subsequently, on the threshold of industrialization and in view of the social and cultural shocks it caused, an explicit Christian Social Ethics helped to gradually bring about important reforms of industrial working and living conditions. Even today, Economy and economic wisdom is not yet at the heard of Christian communities and their preaching. However, Christian Social Ethics represents an established pillar of theological studies in large parts of the Christian cultural sphere. Moreover, engaged lay people inspired by Christian values are participating in the ongoing discussion about a future economy, in which Human life can survive on the planet Earth – and more people can live in Justice and Peace around the Globe. International activities like the Economy of Francisco (https://francescoeconomy.org) – started from engaged leading Western Economists but also reaching out to educate a new generation of academic leaders and Entrepreneurs in Muslim, Buddhist and Hindu countries in Africa and Asia – have to be mentioned here. Initiatives like this represent important testimonies of a global and open ended dialogue between religious and spiritual wisdom traditions on the one hand and economic analysis and knowledge creation on the other.

Bibliography

Acemoglu, Darin/ Robinson, James, *Why Nations Fail. The Origins of Power, Prosperity, and Poverty,* New York: Crown Business, 2012.
Aghion, P. /Antonin, C. / Bunel, S., *The Power of Creative Destruction. Economic Umheaval and the Wealth of Nations*, Cambridge MA: The Belknap Press of Harvard University Press, 2021.
Balthasar, Hans Urs , *Theodramatik*, 4 vols, Einsiedeln: Johannes Verlag, 1976 ff
Balthasar, Hans Urs, *Theologik*. 3 vols, Einsiedeln: Johannes Verlag, 1985 ff.
Berman, Richard, *Law and Revolution, The Formation of the Western Legal Tradition,* Cambridge: Harvard University Press, 1983.

Christensen, Clayton M., *The Innovator's Dilemma: When new technologies cause great firms to fail*, Boston, Massachusetts, USA: Harvard Business School Press, 1997.

CIC 1983 – *The Code of common law*, retrieved from http://www.jgray.org/codes/cic83eng_annotated.html (23.05.2020)

Goldschmidt, N. / Habisch, A., "Western Religion, Social Ethics and Public Economics," in: F. Forte / R. Mudambi / P. Navarra (eds.), *A Handbook of Alternative Theories of Public Economics*, Cheltenham: Elgar, 2014, 198–226.

Habisch, André, "Practical Wisdom for Social Innovation. How Christian Entrepreneurs Triggered the Emergence of the Catholic Social Tradition in Europe," in: J. Backhaus (ed.): *On the Economic Significance of the Catholic Social Doctrine: 125 years of Rerum Novarum*, Cham: Springer 2017, 167–190.

Habisch, André / Loza Adaui, Cristian R., "The Charisma of a Conservative Innovator: Franz Brandts and the Rise of the "Christlich-soziale Bewegung" in Germany in the Age of Industrialization," in: Luigino Bruni / Barbara Sena (eds.), *The Charismatic Principle in Economic and Civil Life: History, Theory and Good Practice*. Florence, n.p. 2011.

Inauen, Emil / Frey, Bruno S. / Rost, Katja / Osterloh, Margit, "Benedictine Tradition and Good Governance." in: Luigino Bruni / Barbara Sena (eds.), *The Charismatic Principle in Social Life*, Routledge Frontiers of Political Economy, London: Routledge, 2012.

Reinert, Hugo / Reinert, Erik S., "Creative Destruction in Economics: Nietzsche, Sombart, Schumpeter," in: J. Backhaus, J. / W. Drechsler (eds.), *Friedrich Nietzsche (1844–1900)*, Cham: Springer 2006, 55–85.

Schallenberg, Peter, "Die franziskanische Spiritualität und eine christliche Moralökonomik (Einführung zur deutschen Ausgabe)," in: Luigino Bruni / Stefano Zamagni (eds.), *Zivilökonomie, Effizienz, Gerechtigkeit, Gemeinwohl* (Christliche Sozialethik im Diskurs 1), Paderborn 2013, 13–29.

Schumpeter, Joseph A., *Capitalism, Socialism and Democracy*, London: Routledge, 1992.

Suggestions for further reading

Oslington, Paul (Ed.), The Oxford Handbook of Christianity and Economics, Oxford University Press 2014.

Oslington, Paul, Political Economy as Natural Theology. Smith, Malthus and Their Followers, Routledge 2017.

Rodney Wilson
The Concept of Economy in Islam

1 Approach

There is an extensive literature on Islamic economics, including historical accounts from the early years of Islam, but most of the writing is contemporary.[1] The aim of this paper is not to provide a chronological history of Islamic economic thought, as there are many such publications, but rather to explore the different subject areas considered to be in the realm of economics from a Muslim perspective. Economics can be defined in terms of a methodology or a subject area, the latter being the approach here, with a discussion of the microeconomics of markets followed by consideration of macroeconomic issues, which have implications for government taxation and spending policies. Self-designated Islamic economists believe that economies should not function in a moral vacuum, but rather that all economic decision making involves moral choices. To guide these choices economists should look at, and be aware of, religious teaching, in the case of Islam the teachings of the Qur'ān and the rulings of *fiqh* jurisprudence. This refers to the writings of Muslim scholars as they interpret and explain the relevance of *Sharī'a* teaching to ever changing economic circumstances.[2] Before this is attempted consideration is given to the distinctive terminology of Islamic economics and the sources it draws from.

2 Islamic Economics and Finance Terminology

In order to understand the fundamental principles of Islamic economics it is crucial to be conversant with the terminology used. All of the terminology is in Arabic, the language of the Holy Qur'ān, the revealed word of Allah. The Qur'ān is

---

[1] El-Ashker, Ahmed / Wilson, Rodney, *Islamic Economics: A Short History*, Leiden: Brill, 2006. Nagaoka, Shinsuke, "Critical overview of the history of Islamic economics: formation, transformation, and new horizons," *Asian and African Area Studies* 11, 2 (2012), 114–136; Islahi, Abdul Azim, *History of Islamic Economic Thought: Contributions of Muslim Scholars to Economic Thought and Analysis*, Cheltenham: Edward Elgar Publishing, 2014.
[2] Kuran, Timur, "The discontents of Islamic economic morality," *The American Economic Review* 86, 2 (1996), 438–442.

Rodney Wilson, Emeritus Professor, Durham University

https://doi.org/10.1515/9783110782486-005

accepted as the definitive source for the terminology and if disputes over meaning arise, Islamic scholars will investigate to determine what verses (*sūra*) from the sacred texts are relevant. The terminology of Islamic economics stands out, not least as it is usually in italics in the text, but is separated from its Arabic roots and possibly corrupted with a change of meaning.

The Qurʿān has been translated into all major languages, but as always with translation precise meanings are often lost and the translation may be a cause of dispute. The term *ribā*, for example, can be translated into English as meaning interest or usury. Islamic economic teaching prohibits *ribā*, but the question arises as to whether this only applies to the excessive interest charges associated with usury, which are widely viewed as exploitative by both Muslims and non-Muslims.[3] Indeed many countries, including secular states, have legislation prohibiting usury. For most advocates of Islamic economics a prohibition of usury is a necessary but not a sufficient condition. Rather all interest receipts and payments are prohibited irrespective of the amount charged. For supporters of Islamic economics *ribā* should be translated as applying to all interest transactions, including usury.[4] Even modest interest receipts and payments are classified as *ribā* and therefore not permitted.

The Qurʿān is explicit in the condemnation of *ribā*, but it is for the faithful to hypothesize on the reasons for the prohibition.[5] This will give the faithful a greater awareness of the evils of sin; in this context what constitutes moral and immoral behavior in economic transactions. It is for the faithful to make the effort (*jihād*) to understand why *ribā* is prohibited. The concept of struggle against the enemies of Islam is not only a military issue, but applies in every sphere, including economics, where immoral behavior is all too prevalent.

2.1 The Importance of Arabic

Although there is writing on Islamic economics in many languages, most of the literature is in Arabic and English. Many Arabic language scholars are also respected for their pronouncements on Islamic economics, and the ability to

---

[3] El-Gamal, Mahmoud A., "An economic explication of the prohibition of Riba in classical Islamic jurisprudence," *Proceedings of the Third Harvard University Forum on Islamic Finance*, 31–44, Cambridge: Center for Middle Eastern Studies, Harvard University, 2000.
[4] Farooq, Mohammad Omar, "The *riba*-interest equation and Islam: reexamination of the traditional arguments," *Global Journal of Finance and Economics* 6, 2 (2009), 99–111.
[5] Samiullah, Muhammad, "Prohibition of *riba* (interest) and insurance in the light of Islam," *Islamic Studies* 21, 2 (1982), 53–76.

read and recite the Qur'ān in its original language is much respected and prized. Historically Arabic language scholarship was seen as complementing research in Islamic economics.

The context has changed dramatically over the last century however, with the spread of Islam world-wide reflecting demographic factors and the success in attracting converts. In the most populous Muslim countries such as Indonesia, Bangladesh and Pakistan Arabic is at best a second language, and often a third language after the local language and English. There may be more Arabic speakers than ever before, but in relative terms the language has declined.

Most of the literature on Islamic economics is in English but Arabic transliterated terms are used to designate economic transactions which are regarded as compliant with *Sharī'a* Islamic law.[6] Consistency is an issue however despite the existence of numerous glossaries, often using different spellings for the transliterated terms.

2.2 *Sharī'a* Scholars and Muslim Economists

In practice this has resulted from two distinctive approaches to Islamic economics. Firstly are the writings of *Sharī'a* scholars, basically linguists, mostly native Arab speakers, but with the ability to read classical Arabic texts.[7] They are not only thoroughly acquainted with the Qur'ān, but with the writings of Islamic scholars, past and present, on economics. However their knowledge of mainstream classical and neoclassical economics is limited; and few have kept up with developments in institutional or behavioral economics which may be relevant to Islamic economics.[8]

The second approach is by trained economic researchers, usually academics, but also including professional economists working for governments or private consultancy firms. Many of these writers have little or no knowledge of Arabic, and struggle to contextualize the terms used for Islamic economic transactions.

Ideally joint publications are a way forward drawing on the skills and expertise both of the economists and the *Sharī'a* scholars. Unfortunately there are no

---

[6] Muqorobin, Masyhudi, "Journey of Islamic economics in the modern world," *Proceedings of The Seventh International Conference on Islamic Economics*, 385–404, 2008.
[7] Siddiqi, M. Nejatullah, "*Sharī'a*, economics and the progress of Islamic finance: the role of *Sharī'a* experts," *Concept Paper presented at Pre-Forum Workshop on Select Ethical and Methodological Issues in Shari'a-Compliant Finance*, Cambridge, Massachusetts, USA, 2006.
[8] Arif, Muhammad, "Toward a definition of Islamic economics: some scientific considerations," *Journal of King Abdulaziz University: Islamic Economics* 2, 2 (1985), 79–93.

examples to date of such collaboration resulting in joint publications as although there are many economists open to the idea of collaborative research this to date appears to be less the case with *Sharī'a* scholars.

3 Source Material and the Conceptualization of Economics in the Sacred Texts of Islam

The Qur'ān is the ultimate source of Islamic teaching on economics as it is the word of Allah.[9] It guides the faithful and provides the parameters for economic decision making.[10] The spiritual determines the material outcomes, not vice versus which results from the worship of false Gods. In the monotheistic religions there is one God to be obeyed and it is sacrilegious to worship material possessions. The duty of the faithful is to abide by and facilitate Allah's Will, and although it is lawful to accumulate possessions, these should be used for the common good rather than personal gratification.[11]

3.1 The *Hadīth*

Although the faithful can read and recite the Qur'ān for themselves, this does not preclude reading other sacred texts which complement and clarify the teaching of the Qur'ān.[12] In particular the *Hadīth*, which record the sayings and deeds of the Prophet, are viewed as an important source for Islamic teaching.[13] These are voluminous, and represent a challenge for believers as it is difficult to know where to start and what to prioritize. The collection of *Hadīth* by Imam Bukhari is widely agreed to be the most important, especially given the pronouncements

---

[9] Choudhury, Masudul Alam, "Principles of Islamic economics," *Middle Eastern Studies* 19, 1 (1983), 93–103.
[10] Presley, John R. / Sessions, John G., "Islamic economics: the emergence of a new paradigm," *The Economic Journal* 104, 424 (1994), 584–596.
[11] Choudhury, Masudul Alam, "Islamic economics as a social science," *International Journal of Social Economics* 17, 6 (1990), 35–69.
[12] Khan, Muhammad Akram, "Methodology of Islamic economics," *International Journal of Economics, Management and Accounting* 1, 1 (1987).
[13] Haneef, Mohamed Aslam, "Islam, the Islamic worldview, and Islamic economics," *International Islamic University Malaysia Journal of Economics and Management* 5, 1 (1997), 39–65.

on honesty in market transactions and the evils of exploitation through monopolistic practices.[14]

3.2 *Fiqh* Islamic Jurisprudence

As the Qur'ān is the word of the Almighty it cannot be challenged by the faithful. This also applies to the *Hadīth* as it is the pronouncements of the Prophet, although there can be discussion about the ranking in importance of *Hadīths*. Islamic jurisprudence (*fiqh*) has a very different status as it is the work of Islamic scholars.[15] *Fiqh* can be criticized and challenged as it is the work of humans, who may make errors and be subject to misunderstandings. Different scholars may have contradictory views on economic issues, but this should be welcomed, not criticized, as debate may result in more persuasive *fiqh* rulings.[16]

Fiqh jurisprudence on economic issues has involved scholarly critiques of changing economic and business practices but the scholars cannot enforce compliance with any recommendations they make at national or international level. Even in countries regarded as theocratic whose governments designate as Islamic, such as the Islamic Republic of Iran or the Islamic Emirate of Afghanistan, the states adhere to secular economic policies and have not attempted to apply specifically Islamic principles. There are no *Sharī'a* governance institutions at national level. Some Muslim majority states countries have ministries of religious affairs, but these seldom get involved in economic policy making.

3.3 *Sharī'a* Governance

Rather than the clergy controlling what governments can do in the economic sphere, it is the governments which exercise control. A typical institution is the Ministry of Islamic Affairs, *Da'wa* and Guidance in Riyadh, a Saudi Arabi-

---

[14] Doniyorov, Alisher Khudoyberdiyevich /Karimov, Nodir Rakhmonqulovich, "An Incomparable Book of a Great Scholar," *Bulletin Social-Economic and Humanitarian Research* 6 (2020), 63–71.
[15] Yusuf Saleem, Muhammad, "Methods and methodologies in *fiqh* and Islamic economics," Research Paper, Department of Economics Kulliyyah of Economics and Management Sciences, International Islamic University Malaysia, 1–17.
[16] Khan, M. Fahim, "Fiqh foundations of the theory of Islamic economics: a survey of selected contemporary writings on economics relevant subjects of fiqh," *Theoretical foundations of Islamic economics* 3 (2002), 59–85.

an government agency established in 1993.[17] It has responsibility for overseeing Islamic affairs, maintaining mosques and supervising King Fahd Complex for the Printing of the Holy Qur'an. Its remit also includes increasing the awareness of good practice in Islam and promoting moderation internationally. Some might see this as a form of censorship. The ministry even distributes sermons, which may make work easier for busy preachers, but also takes away their autonomy and independence.

The ministry is also responsible for supporting the non-profit sector, which in practice involves the administration of *zakāt* and the maintenance of *waqf* endowments. In other words the ministry, as its name implies, facilitates the management of all religious affairs in the Kingdom the main exception being pilgrimage policies which are overseen and administered by the Ministry of *ḥajj* and *ʿumra*.

It is at sector rather than national level where there have been many new texts pertaining to Islamic economics and its sub division, Islamic finance.[18] In particular it has become normal for Islamic financial institutions to appoint *Sharīʿa* boards whose remit is to approve all products offered to clients and monitor all operational processes to ensure they are consistent with Islamic principles.[19] The scholars serving on these boards are appointed by, and responsible to, the board of directors of the financial institutions. In many countries the appointment of *Sharīʿa* boards has become a regulatory requirement enforced by central banks or capital market supervisory authorities. For the clients the *Sharīʿa* boards provides assūrances that their funds are deployed in a manner that avoids *ribā* and are supporting economic activities which are *ḥalāl*, this referring to what is acceptable under Islamic law.[20]

3.4 International Islamic Financial Institutions

There has been much progress internationally in establishing and enhancing standards for *Sharīʿa* governance for Islamic financial institutions. The most no-

---

[17] *Daʿwa* is the act of inviting or calling people to embrace Islam.
[18] Farook, Sayd Zubair / Farooq, Mohammad Omar, "*Sharīʿa* governance for Islamic finance: Challenges and pragmatic solutions," *Available at SSRN 1813483* (2011).
[19] Nawaz, Tasawar / Haniffa, Roszaini /Hudaib, Mohammad, "On intellectual capital efficiency and *Sharīʿa* governance in Islamic banking business model," *International Journal of Finance & Economics* 26, 3 (2021), 3770–3787.
[20] Karbhari, Yusuf / Alam, M. Kausar /Rahman, M. Mizanur, "Relevance of the application of institutional theory in Shariah governance of Islamic banks," *PSU Research Review* (2020), 1–15.

table initiative involved the Kuala Lumpur based Islamic Financial Services Board (IFSB), which was established in 2002 as a standard setting body for Islamic banks, *takāful* Islamic insurance providers and *Sharī'a* compliant Islamic investment funds.[21] It has 187 members including 81 regulatory and supervisory authorities from throughout the Islamic World, as well as other countries where there is substantial Islamic financial activity. The Accounting and Auditing Organization for Islamic Financial Institutions (AAOIFI) was established in Bahrain in 1991, its aim being to ensure that common financial reporting standards are used by Islamic financial institutions.[22] This enables clients and regulators to assess the performance of these institutions in a consistent manner. IFSB and AAOIFI have been supported by the Jeddah based Islamic Development Bank (IsDB) which was founded in 1975 and brings together 57 Muslim majority countries. All of its financing is *Sharī'a* compliant and cumulative funding approvals exceeded US$ 155 billion by the end of the first half of 2021, with the major beneficiaries being Bangladesh, Egypt, Pakistan, Turkey, Morocco and Iran.[23]

4 The Theological and Philosophical Principles of Economics in Islam

A useful starting point to understand the principles of Islamic economics is to examine how it fits in with mainstream economic theory. It is especially rewarding to examine the critiques of the methodological underpinnings of economics from an Islamic perspective.

Contemporary contributors to Islamic economics, notably Umer Chapra (1933–), are critical of conventional classical and neo-classical economic theory, as they are viewed as secular pseudo-sciences without moral underpinnings.[24] They assert that conventional economics elevates the concept of consumer sov-

---

[21] Haron, Abdullah, "Integrating Islamic finance to the global financial system: the role of the Islamic Financial Services Board (IFSB)," *Money and Economy* 7, 1 (2012), 67–85.
[22] Sarea, Adel Mohammed / Hanefah, Mustafa Mohd, "The need of accounting standards for Islamic financial institutions: evidence from AAOIFI," *Journal of Islamic Accounting and Business Research* 4, 1 (2013), 64–76.
[23] Hernandez, Diego / Vadlamannati, Krishna Chaitanya, "Politics of religiously motivated lending: An empirical analysis of aid allocation by the Islamic Development Bank," *Journal of Comparative Economics* 45, 4 (2017), 910–929.
[24] Chapra, M. Umer, "Is it necessary to have Islamic economics?," *The Journal of Socio-Economics* 29, 1 (2000), 21–37.

ereignty above all else.[25] It is consumer preferences which ultimately determine the pattern of economic activity, most notably what is produced and by whom. If income distribution is very uneven and the rich have already many valuable assets, production will be skewed to luxury goods, while the needs of those with little purchasing power are largely ignored. In contrast Islamic economic teaching, according to Umer Chapra , gives priority to basic needs, not wants, where purchases may reflect a desire to impress rather than serve others.[26]

Modern economics adopted Utility theory to explain the behaviour of market participants, the aim being to maximise material satisfaction while minimising dissatisfaction; the so-called calculus of pleasure and pain as proposed by the English philosopher Jeremy Bentham. (1748–1832)[27] Pain was associated with work which involved sacrificing leisure time. For Umer Chapra work, far from being a chore, was seen as serving society and using God given talents productively. Adopting a simplistic hedonistic approach to determining the value of actions was seen as trivialising economic activity through stressing materialism and neglecting the spiritual. Utilitarianism was viewed as being one dimensional and neglecting moral value. What is produced and consumed should be governed by *Sharī'a* teaching rather than being a matter for individual discretion. The aspiration should be to build an orderly and just economy, not to allow a chaotic and selfish society to prevail.

4.1 Sustainability from an Islamic Perspective

Amongst Islamic economists there is growing questioning not only with what is produced, but also of how it is produced. The increased concerns with the sustainability of production and negative environmental consequences for the planet have been taken on board by Islamic economists, not least because many Muslim majority countries have been adversely impacted by climate change, notably the Maldives which may disappear with rising water levels, Bangladesh the victim of ever stronger tropical storms and Jakarta, the largest city in the Muslim

---

[25] Furqani, Hafas, "Consumption and morality: Principles and behavioral framework in Islamic economics," *Journal of King Abdulaziz University: Islamic Economic* 30 (2017), 89–102.
[26] Chapra, M. Umer, *Morality and Justice in Islamic Economics and Finance*, Cheltenham: Edward Elgar Publishing, 2014.
[27] Read, Daniel, "Experienced utility: utility theory from Jeremy Bentham to Daniel Kahneman," *Thinking and Reasoning* 13, 1 (2007), 45–61.

World with over 10 million inhabitants, which is subject to chronic flooding.[28] It is recognised that merely measuring development in terms of gross national product and ignoring environmental and sustainability consequences presents a false picture of what is being achieved economically.[29] A multidisciplinary methodology may be required to provide a more comprehensive picture of the direction in which economies are heading and the wider consequences of supposed economic advance. As Islamic economics involves theology as well as economics a multidisciplinary element is already present.[30]

4.2 Methodical Issues

In 1932 an influential London School of Economics Professor, Lionel Robbins, (1898–1984), defined economics as "the science which studies human behaviour as a relationship between ends and scarce means which have alternative uses".[31] Islamic economists, who were starting to emerge as a separate school of thought at that time, rejected the scarcity theory of Robbins as in Islam followers are taught that Allah has provided resources in abundance for the benefit of mankind. This was contradictory to the secular approach of Robbins, who identified as the major concern of economists whether resource allocation should be left to markets, or alternatively be undertaken by the state. For Islamic economists the hand of Allah was working through his believers in their market actions which were socially beneficial for the most part. Where there were abuses with unfair practices market regulation may be necessary, but not the state taking control of production and rationing consumption.

Islamic economic analysis can accommodate both deductive and inductive methodological approaches. A deductive approach based on logical reasoning is adopted in interpreting the relevance of *Sharī'a* teaching to contemporary conditions, following the path of *fatwa* rulings over the centuries since the time of

---

[28] Hassan, A. B. U. L., "Islamic economics and the environment: Material flow analysis in society-nature interrelationships," *Journal of King Abdulaziz University: Islamic Economics* 18, 1 (2005), 15–31.
[29] Hasan, Zubair, "Sustainable development from an Islamic perspective: meaning, implications, and policy concerns," *Journal of King Abdulaziz University: Islamic Economics* 19, 1 (2006), 3–18.
[30] Wilson, Rodney, 'Economics and morality from an Islamic perspective', In: Hassan, M. Kabir / Lewis, Mervyn K. (eds.), *Handbook on Islam and Economic Life,* Cheltenham: Edward Elgar, 2014, 268–282.
[31] Howson, Susan, "The origins of Lionel Robbins's essay on the nature and significance of economic science," *History of Political Economy* 36, 3 (2004), 413–443.

the Prophet. The alternative inductive approach is empirically based, and can be described as an anthropological investigation, as it focuses on the behaviour of Muslims in their everyday lives, including their work motivation and purchasing decisions. This approach was developed by the Pakistani economist, Syed Naqvi, (1935–)[32] and taken further by Timur Kuran, (1954–), a professor of economics at Duke University, who has studied the behaviour of Muslim minority communities and what he designates as the Islamic sub-economy. [33]

Many contemporary economists see their subject as scientific as theories are tested using empirical data to derive robust conclusions. Findings are supposedly value free, as they result from objective observation rather than subjective judgements. In contrast Islamic economists see subjectivity as acceptable, indeed desirable, as it incorporates a human element rather than being mechanical. Furthermore Islamic economics is seen as prescriptive, indicating what actions should be taken in the light of the religious ideal, rather than being merely descriptive. A similar approach is adopted in modern managerial economics, but this makes no allowances for religion and social culture.

4.3 Distribution in Islamic Economics

The core principles of Islamic economics continue to evolve. Although much of the focus has been on the consequences of the evils of *ribā*, the emphasis is increasingly on the positive implications rather than negative prohibitions. The wider issues are the legitimacy of different types of return, or in other words, justice in remuneration. The concept of a production function is central to economic theory, the basic factors of production being labor, capital and land.[34]

Labor is paid weekly wages or more usually monthly salaries, which are regarded as legitimate earning. Islamic law recognizes private property on which owners earn rents, again a legitimate return under Islamic law.[35] Owners are usually liable for the maintenance of their properties, particular the external struc-

---

[32] Naqvi, Syed Nawab Haider (ed.), *Islam, Economics, and Society (RLE Politics of Islam)*, Routledge, 2013.
[33] Kuran, Timur, *Islam and Mammon: The Economic Predicaments of Islamism*, Princeton University Press, 2004.
[34] Ilmy, Rizky Maidan /Setiawan, Iwan, "The Concept of Production, Distribution, and Consumption in Islamic Economics," *Review of Islamic Economics and Finance (RIEF)* 2, 1 (2019), 41–46.
[35] Wilson, Rodney, "Islam and business," *Thunderbird International Business Review* 48, 1 (2006), 109–123.

ture, while tenants are responsible for interior decoration. Islamic economics permits different types of rental agreement, but these cannot be changed unilaterally and contracts should be transparent and clear for all of the parties. Under Islamic law property is to be used rather than left vacant. Owners are entitled to legitimate rental returns with the amounts related to the market valuation of the assets.

Investors are also able to earn returns under Islamic law which may be in the form of income or capital gains, or both. Investment is only permitted in legitimate activities, with for example prohibitions on funding gambling or the production or distribution of alcohol. Successful investment involves researching the companies being financed which is time consuming. There is always the risk of losses, but this is regarded as legitimizing the investments. Islamic finance offers investment instruments to facilitate profit sharing, which encourages investment in new ventures that might otherwise not be funded.[36] Some of these issues will be explored further when practical applications of Islamic economics and finance are discussed.

4.4 The Prohibition of Interest

In contrast to investment which facilitates risk sharing, opening and maintaining savings accounts in banks paying interest is viewed as undesirable. The returns do not reflect the profitability of what is being funded but rather the cost of debt finance. Defaults are more likely with debt finance as there is nobody to share the burden.[37] Typically banks will charge for loans the going rate paid to savers plus a two or three percent mark-up so that their loans will generate profits for the financial institution. There is no connection between the profitability of the enterprise being funded and the interest rates charged by the bank. Where losses rather than profits arise, borrowers will still be liable for the repayment in full of their debts plus interest charges. Where renegotiation of the terms of loan is allowed it will usually involve a long term increase in the debt in return for a lengthening of the repayments period.

---

[36] Hasan, Zubair, "Risk sharing versus risk transfer in Islamic Finance: a critical appraisal," International *Sharī'a* Research Academy, *(ISRA) International Journal of Islamic Finance* 7, 1 (2015), 7–24.
[37] Bensaid, Benaouda / Grine, Fadila, / Nor, Mohd Roslan Mohd / Yusoff, M. Y. Z. M., "Enduring financial debt: An Islamic perspective," *Middle-East Journal of Scientific Research* 13, (2013), 162–170.

Advocates of Islamic economics believe that it is particularly unfair to have debtors subject to agreements which expose them to interest rate increases that occur when monetary policy is being tightened. In this case macroeconomic developments can bring hardship, whereas it would be more appropriate to have the terms of funding determined at the microeconomic level of individual clients. In the case of residential mortgages those who cannot afford to pay interest charges and repayments may end up being evicted through no fault of their own. Subjecting families to such risks is unacceptable in Muslim society.[38]

5 Market Prices and Transactional Justice

Islamic economists view trading as a legitimate, indeed a desirable economic activity. The Prophet himself was involved in trade, and Mecca and Medina owed their prosperity to being significant markets. The determination of prices by supply and demand forces was regarded as natural, and markets, for the most part, were thought of as functioning efficiently in determining what was produced and consumed.[39] Nevertheless it was recognised that there were cases of market failure, and regulation was necessary to ensure produce was equitably shared and that low income earners were not excluded from the market. Furthermore malpractices could result from unscrupulous trading activity including hoarding to increase prices. Cornering a market by monopolistic practices and speculation was condemned, as was insider trading where information available to some market participants was not shared with others.[40] The quality of what was supplied was also important, including food safety and assurance that meat was certificated as being *ḥalāl*. In the Ottoman Empire the institutional framework for market regulation was through the *ḥisbah*, which comprised Islamic scholars who focused on good and bad practices in market transactions. Market regulation was seen as a moral issue with buying and selling practices subject to *Sharīʿa* law.[41]

---

[38] Shavit, Uriya, "A Fatwa and Its Dialectics: Contextualizing the Permissibility of Mortgages in Stockholm," *Journal of Muslims in Europe* 8, 3 (2019), 335–358.
[39] Islahi, Abdul Azim, "Market Mechanism in Islam: A Historical Perspective," *International Journal of Economics, Management and Accounting* 3, 2 (1995), 1–13.
[40] Al Arif, M. Nur Rianto, "Monopoly and Ikhtikar in Islamic Economics," *Shirkah: Journal of Economics and Business* 1, (2016), 299–310.
[41] Salim, Ssuna / Abdullah, Syahrul Faizaz / Ahmad, Kamarudin, "Wilayat Al-Hisba; a means to achieve justice and maintain high ethical standards in societies," *Mediterranean Journal of Social Sciences* 6, 4 S2 (2015), 201–206.

5.1 Regulation

There remains the question of what market regulation is designed to achieve. Is the moral issue the selfish behaviour of the suppliers which brings their enrichment while their customers are being ripped off through exploitative practices? Alternatively there is the issue of whether the problem is the distribution of income, resulting in some customers lacking the resources to participate in the market, or in other words the problem of financial exclusion, a much discussed issue in Islamic economics.

Ibn Taimīyah (1263–1328) was the first Islamic scholar to examine the workings of markets and consider the implications of the *Sharī'a* for economic policy on trading activity.[42] Much of his life was spent in Damascus, one of the great trading centres of the Muslim World; hence he was well aquatinted with commercial practices. He recognised the workings of supply and demand, with increases in demand causing prices to rise if the supply was fixed, but conversely if the supply increased while demand was static, prices would fall. Such price changes should not be regulated as this could stifle entrepreneurship, and fair profits were viewed as legitimate as long as prices were reasonable. It was only if prices were unjust that regulation was needed, the concept of what constituted a just price being left to the regulator, who would of course listen to customer complaints as well as seller explanations of why prices were rising. In other words the regulator would be involved in arbitration, with *Sharī'a* teaching being that such systems should be fair, but not specifying a particular price, which would depend on economic circumstances. Those working for the *ḥisbah* had considerable power, but this was balanced by social responsibilities which should be exercised in accordance with Islamic teaching. In other words what mattered was process, including providing accurate reporting of the rationale for pricing judgements in a transparent manner.

Ibn Taimīyah's stance on just prices was similar to that of Saint Thomas Aquinas (1225–1274) in Christian writing, and both scholars were familiar with the moral concerns on pricing in ancient Greek philosophy, which undoubtedly influenced their thinking. However contemporary Islamic economists, while respecting the writings of Ibn Taimīyah, have little to say on the morality of pricing, and governments in the Muslim World have largely ignored the issue.[43] The *ḥisbah* was abolished with the demise of the Ottoman Empire and the emergence

---

[42] Khalil, Mohammad Hassan, "Ibn Taymiyyah on reason and revelation in ethics," *Journal of Islamic Philosophy* 2, 1 (2006), 103–132.
[43] Setiawan, Romi Adetio, "The relevance of Ibn Taymiyyah economics in addressing poverty and income distribution," *Madania: Jurnal Kal Kajian Keislaman*, 20, 1 (2016), 13–22.

of the secular Turkish Republic. In the Arab World governments have applied price controls to ensure that basic commodities are affordable for those on low incomes, but this was motivated by the need to avoid street demonstrations and food riots rather than moral concerns.

6 The Historical Evolution of Muslim Perceptions of Economics and Development

Much of contemporary Islamic economics is concerned with the microeconomics of markets rather than macroeconomic policies. The great Islamic philosopher of history, Ibn Khaldūn, (1342–1406) had much wider interests, especially in the area of what is now designated as macroeconomics.[44] His fundamental concern was to analyse the factors explaining the rise and fall of great Empires, as he noted from history that no Empire lasted for ever, but would experience periods of great prosperity and glory, followed by inevitable decline. The contemporary notions of linear development and continuous economic growth were rejected by Ibn Khaldūn given the historical evidence; rather he believed the past experience revealed long term cycles, with the state of the economy and trade determining the strength and weaknesses of the Empires.[45]

6.1 Business Cycles

Ibn Khaldūn identified four stages of the cycle, starting with the expansion phase when peace and order were achieved within the Empire resulting in businesses having the confidence to invest and workers being willing to specialise in the knowledge that their wages and salaries were guaranteed. This notion of specialisation and division of labour was similar to that identified by the Scottish philosopher and economist, Adam Smith (1723–1790), many centuries later when examining the factors explaining the wealth of nations.[46]

---

[44] Boulakia, Jean David C, "Ibn Khaldun: a fourteenth-century economist," *Journal of Political Economy* 79, 5 (1971), 1105–1118.
[45] Spengler, Joseph J., "Economic thought of Islam: Ibn Khaldūn," *Comparative Studies in Society and History* 6, 3 (1964), 268–306.
[46] Ead, Hamed A. and Nada H. Eid, "Between Ibn Khaldun and Adam Smith (Fathers of Economics)," *IOSR Journal of Business and Management* 3 (2014), 54–56.

Essentially what Ibn Khaldūn proposed was a moral theory of the business cycle, as it was anti social behaviour and material greed that resulted in the cyclical downturn.⁴⁷ The vast wealth created in the upswing corrupted the leaders who awarded themselves high salaries and excessive bonuses at the expense of the middle classes and skilled artisans. Increasing income and wealth disparities resulted in social tension and even class warfare and internal revolts. This weakened the state with law and order breaking down. Investors lost confidence, businesses collapsed, government revenue declined and recession, or even depression, ensued. The middle classes and the artisans were economically squeezed and feared not being paid. This was also a concern for the military; they lacked the motivation to defend the state, which risked being invaded and taken over by a stronger country that was able to pursue expansionary policies. Governments which were principled and respected *Sharī'a* survived and prospered, but those behaving in an amoral fashion and worshiping the false material deities collapsed.

Ibn Khaldūn was undoubtedly perceptive and far sighted, and his analysis of economic advance and decline had parallels in Marxian economics.⁴⁸ However Marxism was secularist and ignored, or was openly hostile to, religious values. Marx had no respect for private property, whereas for Islamic economists all property ultimately belongs to Allah, but the faithful have the responsibility for managing property during their lifetimes. There are parallels with the Christian concept of stewardship.⁴⁹

7 The Diversity of Islamic Political, Cultural and Materialistic Contexts

The fifty-seven Muslim majority countries are very diverse in terms of their governance systems, inherited cultural norms and resources, and competency. The Islamic world includes some of the richest countries globally such as Qatar and the United Arab Emirates and some of the poorest, notably Yemen and Af-

---

47 Chapra, M. Umer, "Ibn Khaldun's theory of development: does it help explain the low performance of the present-day Muslim world?" *The Journal of Socio-Economics* 37, 2 (2008), 836–863.
48 Mohammad, Fida, "Ibn Khaldun's theory of social change: a comparison with Hegel, Marx and Durkheim," *American Journal of Islamic Social Sciences* 15, 2 (1998), 25–39.
49 Usman, Abur Hamdi /Ismail, Abu Zaki / Soroni, Mohd Khafidz / Wazir, Rosni, "Rise and Fall of Development: How does Hadith View the Economic System?," *Asian Social Science* 11, 27 (2015), 168–174.

ghanistan. Conflicts, often resulting from sectarian differences, have proved very detrimental to economic development and material advance. Economic and political analysts all too often deplore the paths followed and choices made by citizens of Muslim majority countries and despair for the future. However though it is easy to be influenced by current events, the influence of Islam is best understood and appreciated from a long term perspective. In particular when focusing on economic issues it can be argued that Islam has much to teach secular economic policy makers by providing a spiritual dimension which is ultimately much more important than the exclusively material.

7.1 Trade in Islam

Commitment to the adoption of Islamic economic principles may encourage, perhaps even inspire, greater efforts to improve living standards through an enhanced willingness to participate in economic activity. Trade was critical for the spread of Islam in its early years and attitudes to trade remain favorable in the Muslim World.[50] The Prophet himself was engaged in trade, and Mecca and Medina were important trading centers. The arid lands of the Arabian Peninsula served as conduits for trade, and in contemporary Saudi Arabia and the smaller Gulf states the great trading families have benefited the most from the stimulus to economic activity through oil and gas production.

Qurʿānic teaching stresses the value of trade which is seen as bringing social benefits in contrast to usury that is seen as amoral and selfish.[51] The guidance provided by *sūra* 2:275 is fundamental to Islamic teaching on economic behavior. The faithful are told to rejoice in the bargain they have been able to secure (61:12) through honest trade. However trade should be not at the expense of worship and on Fridays the faithful should focus on prayer rather than being obsessed with making material gains (62:9). It is crucial for believers to have the correct priorities. There is no support in Islam for the notion of only agricultural production or manufacturing being productive while trade is unproductive and adds no value.

An important policy recommendation from Islamic teaching is that free trade should be pursued with economies being opened up rather than embracing protectionism and being isolationist. Inevitably nationalistic policies have

---

[50] Khan, Ajaz Ahmad / Thaut, Laura, "An Islamic perspective on fair trade," *United Kingdom: Islamic Relief* (2008), 1–13.
[51] Khan, Janas / Dad, Karim, "Importance of Commerce and Trade in the Light of the Holy Quran and Sunnah," *Gomal University Journal of Research*, 30, 1 (2014), 131–135.

been pursued in many newly independent Muslim majority countries. This has often taken the form of retaliation to other countries adopting hostile policies, including economic sanctions. From an Islamic perspective tit for tat polices are a move in the wrong direction. The Islamic World was much more connected during the many centuries of Ottoman rule from 1299 until 1922 when the Empire was a free trade area. At the same time there was a degree of local devolution although to ensure stability and order most economic and financial issues were the responsibility of central government. The demise of the Ottoman Empire resulted in economic fragmentation with Britain and France establishing competing spheres of influence that drifted apart. When the British and the French were expelled, tribāl and ethnic divisions were reasserted and became associated with sectarian differences as clergy were associated with particular groups, and none had the charisma and leadership qualities to have a more universal appeal. The Cold War resulted in competition between the United States and the Soviet Union bringing further divisions, with the former focused on the oil rich monarchies whereas the Soviet Union influenced secular republican regimes. The demise of the Soviet Union and the increasing hegemony of the United States failed to serve as unifying influences, possibly because cultural differences were so great and increasing.

The many regional attempts to encourage economic cooperation have ended in failure, starting with the United Arab Republic embracing Egypt and Syria in 1958–1961, which aimed to establish a customs union and common market, influenced by the experience of the European Economic Community (EEC).[52] Unlike the EEC, where sectarian differences were of no relevance, some in Syria saw the alignment with Egypt as boosting the position of local Sunni Muslims as Egypt had an overwhelming Sunni majority. In Syria the Alawites which were to control the country under the Assads, were totally opposed to Nasser's initiatives.

The religious faith of the Alawites is far removed from other Muslims as they believe in reincarnation.[53] As part of their religious ritual they drink wine as a transubstantiated essence, whereas other Muslims abstain from alcohol. Alawites are permitted to drink alcohol at social gatherings, but in moderation. The Alawites share the *Shīʿah* tradition of reverence for Ali, who is considered to be the first Iman of the Twelver school. Ali was a cousin and companion of the Prophet Muhammed. He married the Prophet's daughter Fatimah, becoming

---

52 Palmer, Monte, "The United Arab Republic: an assessment of its failure," *Middle East Journal* 20, 1 (1966), 50–67.
53 Fildis, Ayse Tekdal, "Roots of Alawite-Sunni Rivalry in Syria," *Middle East Policy* 19, 2 (2012), 148–156.

the Prophet's son-in-law. *Shī'ah* adherents to the Twelver School believe that the twelve divinely ordained Imams are the successors to the Prophet, with the last of the twelve reappearing as the promised *mahdī*.[54]

These differences in beliefs are not reflected in economic viewpoints, but they may have minor consequences for economic activity, with for example a famous winery, Domaine de Bargyius, located on the coastal mountains in Latakia. More serious was the widespread feeling that doctorial differences made economic co-operation difficult, if not impossible. The Ottoman Empire tolerated diversity, even if its policies were far from being a celebration of differences. The successor states were, and remain, less tolerant.

Political and economic initiatives such as the founding of the Arab Common Market and the creation of the Arab League had sectarian dimensions.[55] The Arab League was established in 1945 to promote the cause of the Palestinians initially by military co-operation from the six Arab states bordering Israel. The lack of political or military success in preventing the state of Israel being established in 1948 encouraged the Arab League to adopt economic measures to constrain the new state. Subsequently provision for an Arab Common Market was made under a resolution of a proposal by the Economic Council of the Arab League in 1957. This attempted to achieve more positive goals rather than the negativity of sanctions on Israel, which were abandoned in any case as more Arab countries normalized economic relations with the Jewish state. A weakness of the Arab League initiatives was that the countries participating were largely *Sunni* Muslim with Iran excluded because it was not Arab or *Sunni*. Iraq participated as it had a *Sunni* government. However most of Iraq's population was *Shī'ah* and the war with Iran was seen as an aberration. Consequentially Iraq became more accommodating to Iran than to the *Sunni* Arab states, as became soon apparent after the demise of Saddam Hussein.[56]

It is instructive to contrast the workings of the Organization for Islamic Cooperation (OIC) as a more inclusive, belief focused, institution than the Arab League. It was established in 1969 following the attack on the Al-Aqsa Mosque in Jerusalem. Membership comprises 57 Muslim majority countries, including both *Sunni* and *Shī'ah* Muslim states, with the organization based in Jeddah,

---

[54] Ahmad, Saiyad Nizamuddin, "Twelver Šī'ī Ḥadit": from tradition to contemporary evaluations," *Oriente Moderno* 21, 1 (2002), 125–145.
[55] Diab, Muhammad, "The Arab common market," *Journal of Common Market Stud.* 4 (1965), 238–246.
[56] Kontorovich, Eugene, "The Arab League boycott and WTO accession: can foreign policy excuse discriminatory sanctions?" *Chicago Journal of International Law*, 4 (2003), 283.

but Iran as a fully subscribed member.[57] Its most prominent initiative was the founding of the Islamic Development Bank (IsDB) in 1975, also based in Jeddah. It serves as a World Bank for Muslim states with all its financing adhering to Islamic principles. In recent years, in line with international norms, most assistance has been for sustainable development projects with a focus on health and education initiatives as well as infrastructure projects. The IsDB has a proven track record with repayments and an AAA credit rating which enables it to raise low cost funding in addition to members subscriptions.[58]

8 Debates on Economic and Financial Issues within Different Islamic Schools of Thought

There has been a rich debate over the centuries between *Sunni* and *Shī'ah* Islam, and within these traditions further differences of opinion. The majority of Muslims are *Sunni*, around ninety percent, but there are *Shī'ah* minorities in most Muslim countries, and, as already indicated, *Shī'ah* majorities in Iran and Iraq.

The division between *Sunni* and *Shī'ah* primarily concerns governance and the legitimacy of spiritual and political leadership. It is less significant however for economic philosophy as although leading Muslim scholars interested in economics adopt different perspectives; these reflect their own thinking and educational experiences rather than any consensus within *Sunni* or *Shī'ah* Islam. It would be incorrect to speak of a *Shī'ah* school of economic thought, rather there are scholars of Islamic economics who happen to be *Shī'ah* , but this is not the determining factor in their approach to economics.

Similarity although there are four major schools of Islamic thought within Sunni Islam, it would be a mistake to designate the *ḥanafi*, *māliki*, *shāfi'i* or *ḥanbali* schools as being associated with particular approaches to economic analysis or favoring certain economic policies. The scholars serving on the boards of Islamic financial institutions may be very willing, indeed proud, to proclaim their adherence to Abu Ḥanafi, or in the case of Malaysians and Indonesians, allegiance to al-Shāfi'i. This does not preclude board members working alongside those from other traditions. Al Rajhi Bank's *Sharī'a* board for its Malaysian sub-

---

[57] Ahmed, Zahid Shahab / Akbarzadeh, Shahram, "Sectarianism and the Organisation of Islamic Cooperation (OIC)," *Territory, Politics, Governance* 9, 1 (2021), 76–93.
[58] Hernandez, Diego / Vadlamannati, Krishna Chaitanya, "Politics of religiously motivated lending: An empirical analysis of aid allocation by the Islamic Development Bank," *Journal of Comparative Economics* 45, 4 (2017), 910–929.

sidiary is comprised of local scholars in the Shāfi'i tradition. They liaise closely however with the scholars serving on the parent company's *Sharī'a* board in Riyadh who follow the Hanafi tradition. This ensures that a common approach is taken to throughout the international operations of Al Rajhi.

8.1 Economic Dialogue

It is often suggested that the Hanafi approach is stricter than the Shāfi'i but there is no evidence to support this viewpoint as far as Islamic economics or finance is concerned.[59] Being strict has however merits. With *murābaḥah* cost-plus financing in Saudi Arabia the seller and buyer agree to the cost and mark-up on the sale of an asset as a *Sharī'a* compliant method of financing trade. In Malaysia only the purchase price offered by the Islamic bank is disclosed to the seller. This results in non-disclosure of the selling price and a lack of transparency with the mark-up. The argument from the Shāfi'i perspective is that sellers are only interested in the revenue they obtain and the mark-up is a matter for the Islamic bank, not the client.

Similar concerns are expressed in Riyadh about *bai bithaman ajil*, a method of Islamic financing which is not approved off in Saudi Arabia, but is widely used in Malaysia.[60] It is not used however by Al Rajhi Malaysia. *Bai bithaman ajil* is a variant of *murābaḥah*, which is widely used in Saudi Arabia, but *murābaḥah* usually involves payment in installments with the bank having legal rights to the asset and ownership responsibilities which under *Sharī'a* law justifies its remuneration. In contrast *bai bithaman ajil* involves payment in full instantaneously or after a very short time period, and no ownership transfer. The client's motivation for entering into this type of contract is the buyer discount. This is negotiated by the bank with the supplier who may be willing to agree if the bank bulk purchases the good or asset on behalf of several clients.[61]

---

[59] Hayat, Raphie /Den Butter, Frank / Kock, Udo, "Ḥalāl certification for financial products: A transaction cost perspective," *Journal of Business Ethics* 117, 3 (2013), 601–613.
[60] Azli, Rafidah Mohd/ Othman, Rohana / Sahri,Mardiyyah, Nooraslinda, Abdul Aris/ Roshayani, Arshad/ Abdul Razak, Yaakob, "Implementation Of Maqasid Shariah In Islamic House Financing: A Study Of The Rights And Responsibilities Of Contracting Parties In Bai Bithaman Ajil And Musharakah Mutanaqisah," *Journal of Applied Business Research* 27, (2011), 85–96.
[61] Norbaya, Siti,/Abd Hadi Abd Rahman, Muhammad/ Che Yahya, Norliza/ Md Rasid, NorFarah, "Bai Bithaman Ajil (BBA) and Musharakah Mutanaqisah (MM): Comparative Analysis," *Advances in Business Research Journal* 6, 2 (2020), 19–29.

In summary there are three problems with *bai bithaman ajil:* firstly it looks a device without subsistence to circumvent the prohibition of *ribā*; secondly it is complex for the client to understand and third the lack of transparency puts the client at a disadvantage and there is the danger of being ripped off.

The debate over the permissibility of *bai bithaman ajil* demonstrates how differences of perspective can be helpful in the clarification of the issues. Light is also shed on the possible alternatives with implications for policy. This also applies not only within the different traditions amongst *sunni* Islam scholars but at the level of inter sectarian relations to which we should now turn.

8.2 *Shīʿah* Views

There is not a separate school of *Shīʿah* economics but rather a number of influential *Shīʿah* scholars who have made insightful comments on economic issues. Especially notable is the work of Muhammad Baqir Al-Sadr, an Iraqi scholar who was martyred by Saddam Hussein in 1980 together with his sister.[62] Al-Sadr was never sectarian and knew personally senior members of the royal families of Saudi Arabia and Kuwait. He made a positive contribution to *Shīʿah* -*sunni* relations, and his only political involvement was as a founder of the Islamic Dawa Party. Saddam Hussein's accusation that Baqir Al-Sadr was an Iranian agent was untrue.

It is however not his politics, but rather his distinctive contribution to Islamic economics which is the focus here. His greatest writing, *Iqtiṣādunā*, (Our Economy) has been translated into English, and debate on the issues he raised is greater than ever despite it being over forty years since his martyrdom.[63]

Iman Baqir Al-Sadr was primarily a religious scholar, but with a very enquiring intellect and interest in philosophy and social sciences, especially economics. Though not a trained economist he had read widely in political economy, but it was at the interface of theology and economics that he made his greatest intellectual contribution.[64] His key assertion was that economics was a dogma, a system which you either believed or rejected. Those who saw Islamic economics as a science were mistaken; as with religion it was a matter of faith which could

---

[62] Aziz, Talib M., "The role of Muhammad Baqir al-Sadr in Shi'i political activism in Iraq from 1958 to 1980," *International Journal of Middle East Studies* 25, (1993), 207–222.

[63] Aziz, Tareq M., "An Islamic perspective of political economy: The views of (late) Muhammad Baqir al-Sadr," *Al-Tawhid Islamic Journal* 10, (1993).

[64] Furqani, Hafas, "What is Islamic economics? The view of Muhammad Baqir al-Sadr," *Jurnal Ekonomi dan Keuangan Islam* 5, 2 (2019), 63–71.

never be proven.⁶⁵ This insight elevates rather than diminishes the importance of faith, without which our lives are empty. The efficient functioning of the economy fulfils material needs, and riches are viewed as a blessing and not a curse, but what really matters are spiritual aspirations, not material possessions.

Much of the content of *Iqtiṣādunā* consists of a detailed critique of capitalism and communism, both systems he abhors as fundamentally flawed. It is worth mentioning in the context of Iraq that it had by far the largest communist party in the Arab World, although this was persecuted and its members exterminated under the regime of Saddam Hussein. For Baqir Al-Sadr both capitalism and communism are viewed as exploitative and divisive resulting in distraction from the true path of believers towards spiritual fulfilment. In contrast an Islamic economy, guided by scripture, would be harmonious, creating opportunities for meaningful common worship at a deeper level. There would be no need to worry about material security, as the world which Allah provided for the benefit of the faithful would provide for human needs with abundance.

Baqir Al-Sadr was not only interested in economic theory but also in economic policy issues.⁶⁶ He appreciated the benefits and costs of having economies dominated by oil which applied in both Iraq and Iran. When investigating what the role of the state should be in the economy Baqir Al-Sadr envisages most production being undertaken by the private sector with significant funding and control by the state of sectors such as education and health care. He viewed oil as a unique asset, but also as a potential liability, which should not be part of either the private or nationalised sector. Rather it should be within a sector of its own, which could be designated as a state sector, but whose remit included not simply production but rather governance of oil sector assets in the interest of the whole population. The role he envisaged was similar to that of a sovereign wealth fund, but his untimely death meant he did not live to see how such funds worked in practice.

Baqir Al-Sadr's interests included Islamic banking which he wrote about separately to the *Iqtiṣādunā*. In 1974 he attended the early conferences in Jeddah on Islamic banking at the time the Islamic Development Bank was being established. He was approached by the governor of the Central Bank of Kuwait to prepare a report on the establishment of an Islamic bank in the Emirate, a mission which he was pleased to take-on. His plan resulted in the establishment of the Kuwait Finance House in 1977 which has since expanded beyond Kuwait to be-

---

65 Wilson, Rodney, 'The contribution of Muhammad Baqir Al-Sadr to contemporary Islamic economic thought', *Journal of Islamic Studies*, 9, 1 (1998), 46–59.
66 Al-Rikabi, Jaffar, "Baqir al-Sadr and the Islamic State: A Theory for 'Islamic Democracy'," *Journal of Shi'a Islamic Studies* 5, (2012), 249–275.

come one of the largest Islamic financial institutions globally with branches throughout Turkey and a significant presence in South East Asia.[67]

8.3 Iranian Differences

The other well known senior *Shī'ah* researcher in the fields of Islamic economics and finance is Abohassan Banisadr, who was the first President of the Islamic Republic of Iran following the overturn of the monarchy in 1979 and the flight of the King into exile.

Banisadr was a trained economist with an interest in Islamic economics, but he was more concerned with economic policy making than theory. His success with his studies however resulted in him being admitted to the doctoral program at the Sorbonne University in Paris. Islamic economics was his chosen PhD topic which he worked on in the 1970s, with the complication of his thesis and graduation just shortly before the Iranian revolution. In Paris, despite his young age, he became a confident of the supreme spiritual leader, Ayatollah Khomeini who lived in exile at Neauphle-le-Château, outside Paris.

Banisadr's lasting legacy was the conversion of the entire banking system in Iran to being *Sharī'a* compliant. He started the process off, but there was a three year preparation period before the Law on *ribā* free banking was applied in 1983. In other Muslim majority states Islamic banks have to compete with conventional banks offering interest based savings accounts and financing facilities. Iran is the only Muslim country to use Islamic financial contracts for all financial dealing.[68] Other countries, notably Pakistan and the Sudan, have aspired to bring this transformation, but only Iran has implemented *Sharī'a* compliance measures on a sustainable basis.[69] It should be stressed however that the transformation in Iran is not because of *Shī'ah* beliefs, but because of the particular situation in the country and its recent economic history.

---

67 Al Noumani, Dalal/ Al Mutairi, Fawaz/ Machado, Julian, "Kuwait Finance House," *International Journal of Accounting & Finance in Asia Pasific* 2, (2019), 1–4.
68 Ashraf, S. Husain / Giashi, Ali Alizadeh, "Islamic banking in Iran: Progress and challenges," *Kuwait Chapter of Arabian Journal of Business and Management Review* 33, 830 (2011), 1–28.
69 Anwar, Muhammad, "Islamic banking in Iran and Pakistan: a comparative study," *The Pakistan Development Review* 31, 4 (1992), 1089–1097.

9 Possible Dialogical Elements, Differences and Overlaps of the Concept in Relation to the Other Two Monotheistic Religions

There has been a substantial increase in inter-faith dialogue on economics over the last fifty years driven partly by the growing diversity of economic enquiry and the willingness to explore interdisciplinary frontiers including that between economics as a subject discipline and theology.[70] At the same time the great monotheistic religions, Judaism, Christianity and Islam, have increasingly looked outward, partly due to the efforts of the Roman Catholic Church after the Second Vatican Council of 1965 which made historic changes to church policies and theology. An important aim was to facilitate discussion between Christians and those of other faiths, including in the sphere of economics.

The new approach was spelt out in a document, *nostra aetate,* Latin for "In Our Time." Rather than perpetuate suspicions of other religions and antagonisms resulting from historical conflicts, the new approach was for the representatives of the monotheistic faiths to learn from each other in an atmosphere of mutual respect.[71] Religion was often a divisive factor in economic history but by studying past experiences faults and mistakes can be recognised with the parties moving to a fresh start.[72]

Each faith faced similar challenges to which they had to respond, but they could learn from each other's experiences which could strengthen rather than weaken their dealings with secular authority. The objective of dialogue was not to reach agreement on common positions, but rather to be aware of what the representatives of each faith were advocating with respect to economic questions such as income and wealth distribution or sustainable development. Moral principles and practices are very important from a religious perspective which provides a foundation for the discussion of issues such as ethical finance and the treatment of debtors. The Old Testament concept of debt forgiveness in the context of a jubilee could well be part of the discussion. Jews, Christians and Muslims are fully aware of their differing positions on interest based transac-

---

[70] Wilson, Rodney, *Economics, Ethics and Religion: Jewish, Christian and Muslim Economic Thought,* London: Palgrave Macmillan, 1997.
[71] Krokus, Christian S, "Catholic Saints and Scholars: Nostra Aetate and Islam," in: Ellis, Kail C. (ed.), *Nostra Aetate, Non-Christian Religions, and Interfaith Relations,* 115–137, Cham: Palgrave Macmillan, 2021.
[72] Becker, Sascha O. / Rubin, Jared / Woessmann, Ludger, "Religion in economic history: A survey," *The Handbook of Historical Economics* (2021), 585–639.

tions, but rather than avoiding dialog because some see the topic as sensitive, the issue is best approached as a quest for understanding.[73]

Increasingly global developments bring the faithful together in prayer and discussion. The response to the Covid-19 pandemic is an example of this, with religious leaders stressing the importance of the poor being vaccinated in the interest of their own health and that of their dependents.[74] There is also the argument that unless the virus is eliminated as far as possible world-wide it will always re-occur, as rich countries cannot isolate themselves from the rest of the world.

There are some positive benefits however. The restrictions on international travel create time for prayer and meditation, and inter-faith solidarity is achieved through these means rather than physical contacts. The virus does not discriminate between different religions: all are vulnerable. Jews, Christians and Muslims have to obey public health orders which profoundly affect the form of their religious services. Face masks and social distancing measures have to be accepted even though they negatively affect the religious experience. Fortunately humans are adaptable, and their religious beliefs can help enormously in times of difficulty. On a practical level economic and financial issues can also be discussed in the context of maintaining places of worship, as Covid-19 has negatively impacted on the income of synagogues, churches and mosques.

There are a number of forums where academic papers are presented on Christianity and Economics. These include the United Kingdom based Association of Christian Economist and its United States sister organisation. Both host papers on comparative religious perspectives on economics.[75] In Israel researchers at Bar Ilan University, Ramat Gan, have undertaken work on Judaism from an economic perspective. Carmel Ullman Chiswick of George Washington University has been active in this area, but looking at how economic choices influence Judaism rather than vice versa.[76] For work on Islam and economics the oldest established centre is at King Abdulaziz University in Jeddah. It hosts a journal published in English twice a year with an Arabic edition once a year. It was first

---

[73] Calder, Ryan, "God's Technicians: Religious Jurists and the Usury Ban in Judaism, Christianity, and Islam," *European Journal of Sociology/Archives Européennes de Sociologie* 57, 2 (2016), 207–257.

[74] Elsanousi, Mohamed/ Visotzky,Burton L. / Roberts, Bob, "Love your neighbour: Islam, Judaism and Christianity come together over COVID-19," Western Michigan University, 2020.

[75] Wilson, Rodney,"Comparative religious thought on economic behaviour and financial transactions," *Association of Christian Economists Journal* 23, (1997), 1–10.

[76] Chiswick, Carmel Ullman, *Judaism in Transition: How Economic Choices Shape Religious Tradition*, Stanford University Press, 2014.

published in 1983 and is now assisted by the international academic publishing house, Elsevier.[77]

For inter-faith dialogue the Jewish, Christian, Muslim (JCM) conference provides a forum for academic discussion and feedback for researchers working on particular aspects of economics and religion. The theme of the JCM Conference in February 2022 was: *Stewards of the Earth – Religious Responses to Climate Change and its Consequences*. The annual conferences are usually held in Haus Wasserburg, Vallendar.[78]

10 The Current State of Research in Islamic Economics and Interfaith Exchanges between Communities of Believers

There are hundreds of academic researchers working on topics in Islamic economics and thousands specializing in Islamic finance. The subject has taken off since the 1970s and there are now more active researchers than there were in the first 1,400 years of Islam. Although there have been funding initiatives by some governments and the Islamic Development Bank (IsDB) has provided scholarships, the enormous expansion reflects the enthusiasm and commitment of students to Islamic economics and finance. The momentum is coming from the graduate population, and it can be described as a bottom-up movement rather than a top-down initiative from governments.[79]

It is also notable that large numbers of women are studying and researching in Islamic economics and finance, even though mainstream economics and finance are overwhelmingly dominated by men. Around forty percent of the M.Sc. and doctoral students are women, and perhaps ten percent of the academic staff. The proportion of women is highest in Malaysia and Indonesia, but the numbers are increasing in the Gulf, especially in Qatar and UAE, where in the University of Sharjah women account for the majority of students on the MBA program in Islamic finance.

The majority of academic researchers in Islamic economics and finance are employed in business schools, many of which include departments of econom-

---

[77] Wilson, Rodney, "The application of Islamic thought to economic policy making in a threatened world", *Journal of Islamic Economics*, 34, 2 (2021), 157–162.
[78] https://www.jcmconference.org/
[79] Nu'Man, Ruqiyyah, / Ali, S. Nazim, "Islamic economics and finance education: consensus on reform," *Journal of Faculty of Islamic Studies-Hamad Bin Khalifa University* (2016), 76–97.

ics. These researchers' qualifications and training has been in economics. Within institutes of Middle Eastern Studies there are also active researchers of Islamic economics. Some of these institutes offer courses on Arabic and other Middle Eastern languages. Researchers in Islamic studies departments often include Islamic economics in their remit, with some having a background in *fiqh* rather than economics. In the Faculty of Islamic Studies in Qatar there is a team of researchers working on Islamic economics and finance topics.

The International Center for Education in Islamic Finance (INCEIF) in Kuala Lumpur, which is part funded by the Malaysian Central Bank, is the world's largest centre for research in Islamic economics and finance. Finally there are a small number of lone academics in departments of politics and law, with the former specializing in Islamic political economy and the latter focused on Middle Eastern commercial law rather than *fiqh*. Departments or schools which employ a single researcher in Islamic economics are obviously vulnerable in fulfilling their commitments if the staff member is indisposed. Applicants for academic courses and degrees in Islamic economics should bear this in mind.[80]

There are many opportunities for interfaith exchanges between communities of believers through workshops, seminars and conferences. The main annual conferences in Islamic finance are commercial rather than academic and are held in business centers such as Dubai. Since the pandemic most of the conferences have become virtual. This has resulted in the number of participants actually rising, although networking becomes less satisfactory. The most popular venues for international conferences in Islamic economics have been Turkey, Malaysia and Pakistan but there have also been many conferences over the years in London.

11 An Outline of Contemporary Practical Applications of Islamic Economics and Finance

Economic policy making throughout the Islamic World has been and remains essentially secular and little different to that of other countries. Historically this was explained by the weak position of Muslim majority countries where the economic agenda was determined by European colonial powers in the nineteenth and early twentieth century and by the United States in the later twentieth cen-

---

[80] Belabes, Abderrazak / Belouafi, Ahmed / Daoudi, Mohamed, "Designing Islamic Finance Programmes in a Competitive Educational Space: The Islamic Economics Institute Experiment," *Procedia-Social and Behavioral Sciences* 191 (2015), 639–643.

tury. Economic power is evolving rapidly with the rise of China and India, although Muslim countries have reservations about these developments as both countries have Muslim minorities, not majorities, and there has been a history of conflict involving their religious communities.

However, the changing international economic landscape offers opportunities for some Muslim countries. In particular the Group of Twenty (G20) industrialized nations includes three Muslim majority countries, Turkey, Saudi Arabia and Indonesia. They have a platform in this group of the world's leading economies if they choose to use it to advance awareness of Islamic economics. To date there has been no coordination between these three countries and the subject of Islamic economics has not arisen. Nevertheless knowledge of the practical applications of Islamic economics is spreading, especially in the fields of banking, insurance and the management of investment funds.

11.1 Islamic Banking Models

Islamic banking emerged in the 1960s in Egypt and Pakistan as a result of private, voluntary initiatives. In Egypt a doctoral student, Ahmed El Najjar, who won a scholarship to research in Germany, was impressed by the policies of local savings banks.[81] Although they were involved in interest transactions, the amounts were minimal, the major feature which impressed El Najjar was the mutual trust of the clients and management and the strong connections with their local communities in Germany. On his return to Egypt he opened and managed a small savings bank in 1963 in the town of Mitr Ghams in the Nile delta. The venture was very successful in harnessing funds from landowners and small traders who had hitherto not used banks, as they were devout Muslims who were concerned about any dealings involving *ribā*. Within three years more than 60,000 Muslims had deposits with the bank.[82] The bank was based on mutual help, as depositors received no interest, but their deposits qualified them for interest free loans. In traditional *fiqh* these were classified as *qarḍ ḥasan* loans, the only type of loan permissible under *Sharī'a*.[83] The Egyptian government was suspicious of the bank, and allegations were made that many of its clients were mem-

---

[81] Mayer, Ann Elizabeth, "Islamic Banking and Credit Polices in the Sadat Era: The Social Origins of Islamic Banking in Egypt," *Arab Law Quarterly* 1, 1 (1985), 32–50.
[82] Wilson, Rodney, *Economic Development in the Middle East*, 3rd edition, London and New York: Routledge, 2022, 113–114.
[83] Abdullah, Mohammad, "Analysing the moral aspect of qard: a shariah perspective," *International Journal of Islamic and Middle Eastern Finance and Management* 8, 2 (2015), 171–184.

bers of the Muslim Brotherhood, which under Egyptian law was an illegal organisation. Subsequently in 1971 the bank was nationalised and put under government control. It was renamed as the Nasser Social Bank and its rural focus was maintained, but it no longer stressed its Islamic credentials.

With the oil boom of the 1970s the focus of Islamic finance moved to the Gulf where the business community was interested in the notion of *Sharīʿa* compliant finance and potentially to using the services offered by Islamic banks.[84] Subsequently the Dubai Islamic Bank opened in 1975 as the world's first Islamic commercial bank. Rather than being based on a mutual structure of the type adopted in Egypt and Pakistan, the Dubai Islamic Bank was established as a limited liability company with shareholders who hoped to make profits and capital gains from their investment. The founders were mostly successful trading families and companies who required import finance which they were willing to pay for. Initially Dubai Islamic Bank was a private equity company, but in 2000 it became public listed company with the opening of the Dubai Financial Market. There has been active trading of its stock since then with most of its investors being private families rather than institutional investors.[85] Given the limitations of the Dubai market, Dubai Islamic Bank has established wholly owned subsidiaries in Pakistan and Kenya. Migrants from these countries working in the United Arab Emirates can send remittances at minimal costs to their families through transfers within the bank. Many expatriates use funding accumulated from their salaries in the Gulf to extend or rebuild their family homes back in their countries of origin. As Dubai Islamic Bank will have information on their salaries and credit scores vetting costs to approve mortgage applications are minimised, and there is less risk for the bank.[86]

11.2 Methods of Financing

Although much of the business of the Dubai Islamic Bank today is accounted for by personal retail banking corporate finance remains important, especially trade

---

[84] De Belder, Richard T. / Khan, Mansoor Hassan, "The changing face of Islamic banking," *International Finance Law Review* 12 (1993), 23–29.
[85] Al-Tamimi, Hussein A. Hassan / Al-Amiri, Abdullah, "Analysing service quality in the UAE Islamic banks," *Journal of Financial Services Marketing* 8, 2 (2003), 119–132.
[86] Rehman, Asma Abdul/ Masood, Omar, "Why do customers patronize Islamic banks? A case study of Pakistan," *Qualitative Research in Financial Markets* 4.2, 3 (2012), 130–141.

finance based on the principal of *murābaḥah*.[87] Under these contracts the bank purchases imports on behalf of their clients and re-sells them to the clients for a profit mark-up. The profit margin depends on the terms of the transaction rather than interest. The bank can negotiate discounts on the goods supplied by the exporter as there is less risk of a bank rather than a trader defaulting. Furthermore if the bank is serving several trading companies it may be able to bulk purchase, obtaining even deeper discounts. In addition a layer of cost may be eliminated as exporters usually require importers to take-out export credit insurance to guarantee the payments. When banks make the payment these safeguards become unnecessary.

Given these advantages it is unsurprising that *murābaḥah* contracts have become the dominant financing business of Islamic banks. The contract is *Sharī'a* compliant as it involves risk sharing between the bank and the client. The bank must own the goods being financed, albeit on a very short term and temporary basis. This ownership justifies the bank's profit mark-up under Islamic law, as the contract is classified as a trading transaction, not an interest based financing operation.[88]

Most *murābaḥah* contracts are of short term duration, financing for days or a month, but not a year. Originally repayment would be by a single cash transfer but in recent years payments through instalments have proved increasingly popular. However extending the time period for a *murābaḥah* contract may introduce or increase risks for all parties without appropriate safeguards. With Islamic finance it is important to use the relevant contract for the correct purpose. Where repayments are scheduled for two to five years, an *ijārah* leasing contract may be more appropriate than a *murābaḥah* contract given the longer time period.[89] With *murābaḥah* contracts the concern is with the delivery of the asset to the buyer. The bank as buyer has a responsibility to ensure the assets are as specified. *Murābaḥah* is however like a snap shot as once the asset passes to the buyer the bank has no further responsibility. In contrast with *ijārah* the bank, as owner, will have some responsibility for the maintenance of the asset. In other words the lease holder will benefit from the contractual terms of the lease.

---

[87] Sairally, Beebee Salma, "*Murabahah* financing: Some controversial issues," *Review of Islamic Economics* (2002), 73–86.

[88] Ismal, Rifki, "Assessing moral hazard problem in *Murabahah* financing," *Journal of Islamic Economics, Banking and Finance* 5, 2 (2009), 101–112.

[89] Lateef, Adeyemo Wale/ Abdurrazzaq, Alawiye Abdulmumin/ Abdul Shukor, Syahirah/ Ahmad Tajudin, Amalina, "Maqasid Al-Sharī'a in Ijarah (Leasing) Contract of Islamic Banking System," *Journal of Islamic Finance* 6, 2 (2017), 38–44.

It is also worth mentioning that there is a higher purchase variant, *ijārah wa iqtina*, on some leasing contracts. Under such contracts the ownership of the asset passes to the lessee at the end of the lease period, usually after an additional payment is made. These provisions can be included in the initial contract or alternatively offered as an option with no commitment or payments obligation by the lessee until the end of the period of the lease. *Ijārah wa iqtīna* is most common when the assets are real estate or buildings but for transport equipment and machinery lessees may not want ownership as by the end of the lease period new more technologically advanced equipment may have become available.[90]

Islamic financing is particularly well suited for long term funding such as mortgages on residential or commercial property. Although *murābaḥah* and *ijārah* contracts are offered by some Islamic banks to mortgage applicants there are much more suitable contracts available, notably those based on *mushārakah*.[91] The latter is based on co-ownership with the Islamic bank and its client signing a partnership contract. Typically the bank will advance at least 80 percent of the cost of the property while the client contributes 20 percent. The client pays rent to the bank proportionate to the bank's stake in the ownership of the property. The client also makes repayments to the bank often for a 10 year period but sometimes for as long as 20 or even 30 years.

There has been a need for flexibility in the timing of repayments to help market Islamic mortgages and to ensure they are on terms which are competitive with interest based mortgages. As debts to Islamic banks will be highest at the start of the mortgage period this could result in the initial rental payments being maximised. In other words rental payments would be front loaded. In practise mortgages are usually back loaded with higher rents as the end of the mortgage period approaches. This makes the mortgages more affordable as the clients may earn more in the long run with career development and promotion.[92]

Qatari owned Al Rayan Bank, which is the leading Islamic bank in London, offers five year fixed rental payments of less than 3 percent to credit worthy applicants seeking to purchase houses in the United Kingdom. Al Rayan has over

---

90 Billah, Mohd Ma'Sum, "Islamic Leasing Leading to Ownership (Al-Ijarah Tantahi Bi Al-Tamleek)," *Islamic Financial Products*, Cham: Palgrave Macmillan, 2019, 243–254.
91 Muhammad, Abid Mahmood, "Critical analysis of some of the major internal hindrance factors in the application of *Musharakah* financing by the Islamic banks," *International Journal of Education and Research* 2, 9 (2014), 125–142.
92 Matthews, Robin/ Tlemsani, Issam / Siddiqui, Aftab, "Recent developments in the market for Islamic mortgages: Theory and practice," *Review of Islamic Economics* 14 (2003), 49–68.

90,000 customers, mostly United Kingdom passport holders, but also including Gulf based Arabs with residency rights in the United Kingdom.[93]

11.3 Islamic Bank Deposits

Most deposits with Islamic banks are in transaction accounts where they are used to make everyday payments, mostly by on-line transfers. As is the case with conventional banks no interest is paid to these depositors. For personal customers salaries, social benefits or pensions are paid each month into their bank accounts which are used to pay for household expenditures. For business customers deposits come from clients paying for services which the businesses provide. Islamic banks use national and international payments systems to deposit and receive money from other banks, including interbank clearing systems with identifiers such as BIC SWIFT codes[94] or International Bank Account Numbers (IBAN). There are no reservations from a *Sharī'a* perspective concerning the use of these systems.

Savings accounts in Islamic banks are totally different however to those in conventional banks which pay interest to depositors. When monetary policy is tightened and interest rates rise, depositors will receive income gains. With monetary easing interest rates fall and depositors may suffer losses. These gains and losses cannot be justified from a *Sharī'a* perspective.[95] Rather than having savings deposits based on *ribā* Islamic banks offer investment accounts where depositors benefit from the profits generated from their investments.[96] These deposits are designated as *muḍārabah* profit sharing accounts. They can be unspecified, where the profit shares paid to depositors are dependent on the profitability of the Islamic bank, or restricted where the amount of profit paid depends on the return from the specific project which the deposit finances. The latter tends to be more risky with volatile returns.[97]

---

[93] Tameme, Mohammed /Asutay, Mehmet, "An empirical inquiry into marketing Islamic mortgages in the UK," *International Journal of Bank Marketing* (2012), 49–68.
[94] Society for Worldwide Interbank Financial Telecommunications (SWIFT)
[95] Abduh, Muhamad/ Azmi Omar, Mohd, / Duasa, Jarita. "The impact of crisis and macroeconomic variables towards Islamic banking deposits," *American Journal of Applied Sciences* 8, 12 (2011), 1413–1418.
[96] Yusoff, Remali/ Wilson, Rodney, "An econometric analysis of conventional and Islamic bank deposits in Malaysia," *Review of Islamic Economics* 9, 1 (2005), 31–52.
[97] Akhtar, Beenish/ Akhter, Waheed /Shahbaz, Muhammad, "Determinants of deposits in conventional and Islamic banking: a case of an emerging economy," *International Journal of Emerging Markets* 12, 2 (2017), 296–309.

It should be noted that traditional *muḍārabah* partnership agreements provided for both profit and loss sharing. However since the 1970s when Islamic banks were established as limited liability companies it is the shareholders that can suffer losses, not the depositors. In times of financial stress the value of the bank shares will usually decline, with the shareholders facing capital losses. The worst scenario for the depositors is that they will not receive any profits.

11.4 Islamic Insurance

The *takāful* Islamic insurance business has grown rapidly since the 1980s, especially in Saudi Arabia and the states of the Gulf, as well as having a significance presence in Malaysia. There are three factors which potentially make conventional insurance incompatible with Sharīʿa law. First conventional insurance is seen as a form of gambling, (*maysir*) as the premiums amount to bets as payment is dependent on specific event. Insurance payouts are contingent on outcomes that are unknown when the contract is signed. Contractual uncertainty (*gharar*) is regarded as contrary to Islamic law.[98] Conventional insurance contracts are criticised as misleading, using legal jargon with the conditions all too often hidden in the small print.[99] *Takāful* products have to be approved by a *Sharīʿa* board serving the insurance company. The board expects honest and full disclosure of the terms and conditions with the contracts being transparent and understandable to the clients.[100]

Secondly there is concern over the financial assets held by insurance companies. Corporate and sovereign bonds account for a major proportion of their investment portfolio, but these pay interest. Alternative investment in property and equities can of course be *Sharīʿa* compliant but from a financial perspective they have major limitations. Property investment is often illiquid and equity prices fluctuate to a much greater extent than bonds. For *takāful* operators the solution is to invest in *Sharīʿa* approved *ṣukūk*, which are structured like bonds but

---

[98] Cattelan, Valentino, "From the concept of haqq to the prohibitions of riba, gharar and maysir in Islamic finance," *International Journal of Monetary Economics and Finance* 2, 3–4 (2009), 384–397.
[99] Mihajat, Muhammad Iman Sastra, "Contemporary practice of Ribā, Gharar and Maysir in Islamic banking and finance," *International Journal of Islamic Management and Business* 2, (2016), 1–19.
[100] Maysami, Ramin Cooper/ Kwon, W. Jean, "An Analysis of Islamic Takaful Insurance," *Journal of Insurance Regulation* 18, 1 (1999), 109–133.

pay rental income or profit shares rather than interest. The characteristics of *ṣukūk* will be examined more fully in the section on Islamic capital markets.

The third concern with conventional insurance is that if it is offered by a limited liability company there are inherent conflicts of interest between the compensation payments to the clients and shareholder remuneration. The higher the value of successful claims paid by the company the lower the shareholder dividends. Many *Sharī'a* scholars advocate all insurance providers being mutual organisations rather than limited liability companies. The term *takāful* is derived from the root word *kafala* which means to guarantee. *Takafala* means to mutually guarantee its origins being solidarity and mutual help, *takāful ijtima'*, the Qur'ānic term being "*ta'āwun*" (Sūra 5:2), compensation. In a mutual organisation the clients are the sole stakeholders and there are no shareholders. This avoids conflicts of interest.

Although the clients join the *takāful* to obtain personal or family insurance the premiums they pay benefit all *takāful* participants. In other words the participants are socially motivated and are not simply protecting their own interest. There is a sense that they are bearing each other's burden as part of a community. This contrasts with conventional insurance where the clients pay their premiums for their own benefit, not for the benefit of others.[101] The Takāful Act of Malaysia (1984) defines Islamic insurance as "a scheme based on brotherhood, solidarity and mutual assistance, which provides financial aid and assistance to the participants in the case of need whereby the participants mutually agree to contribute for the purpose. The premiums paid can be regarded as donations, the Arabic concept being *tabarru*, which refers to charitable giving. In other words the clients make an unconditional gift without recourse.[102]

Supporters of *takāful* are aware that de-mutualisation has become a feature of conventional insurance markets since the 1960s. There has been much debate about the limitations of mutual organisations, notably that they can only raise capital internally by recourse to members or by borrowing. In contrast de-mutualisation can bring in external capital from equity investors. This may result in an ability to expand and provide more attractive and better paid positions for managers.

---

[101] Hussain, Mher Mushtaq / Pasha, Ahmad Tisman, "Conceptual and operational differences between general *takaful* and conventional insurance," *Australian Journal of Business and Management Research* 1, 8 (2011), 23–28.
[102] Ali, M. Mahbubi / Hassan, Rusni / Hasan, Shabana M., "An exploratory study of Sharī'a issues in the application of *Tabarru'*for *takaful*," *Global Review of Islamic Economics and Business* 1, 3 (2015), 164–174.

There are two alternative methods of organising *takāful* providers to make it more attractive from a management perspective. First is the *wakala* trust model where fees deducted from profits generated from invested funds cover management salaries and expenses.[103] Second is the *muḍārabah* model where operator entitled to a fixed percentage of any profits generated by *takāful* fund. The latter provides more management incentive for long term policies such as those providing for mortgage protection. In the event of the death of the head of the household the policy will pay-off the remainder of the mortgage owed. This is called family *takāful*, which is a pre-condition for an Islamic mortgage being approved.[104] Family protection policies can run for 20 years or more in contrast to medical, vehicle or travel *takāful* which is subject to annual renewal.[105] Usually these are organised using a *wakala* model with management remuneration paid from the annual fees.

11.5 *Sharīʿa* Compliant Fund Management

The development of Islamic finance has not only brought innovative bank and insurance provision but also tools to facilitate *Sharīʿa* compliant investment. This can be through *ṣukūk* issuance, which will be considered in the next section, or fund management institutions, which will be considered here. The enormous range of investment funds available has been replicated by Islamic funds, with for example, open ended funds offered for buying and selling throughout the trading day, in contrast to closed funds which when fully subscribed cannot be bought by outsiders.[106] Furthermore closed ended funds are often illiquid, with no sales permitted during the first or second year after issuance. Investors who are locked out of the market in tradable securities will, of course, expect higher returns as compensation for the loss of liquidity. As stock market devel-

---

[103] Hamid, Mohamad Abdul, "*Sharīʿa* compliance of *wakalah* concept in *Takaful* operation: A case study of a *Takaful* operation in Malaysia," *Tazkia Islamic Finance and Business Review* 8, 2 (2014), 1–26.
[104] Redzuan, Hendon/ Abdul Rahman, Zuriah/ Aidid, S. S. S. H., "Economic determinants of family *takaful* consumption: Evidence from Malaysia," *International Review of Business Research Papers* 5, 5 (2009), 193–211.
[105] Yazid, Ahmad Shukri / Arifin, Juliana / Hussin, Mohd Rasid / Wan Daud, Wan Norhayate, "Determinants of family *takaful* (Islamic life insurance) demand: a conceptual framework for a Malaysian study," *International Journal of Business and Management* 7, 6 (2012), 115–127.
[106] Charfeddine, Lanouar / Najah, Ahlem / Teulon, Frédéric, "Socially responsible investing and Islamic funds: New perspectives for portfolio allocation," *Research in International Business and Finance* 36 (2016), 351–361.

opment in much of the Islamic World is limited, there is greater reliance on private equity finance raised through closed ended funds.

The investment opportunities which managed funds provide have been replicated for Islamic funds. What is different with Islamic funds are the targets for investment, as they are all subject to a screening process to ensure *Sharī'a* compliance.[107] There are two types of screen, financial and business activity. The financial screens are precautionary, and were introduced to limit leveraging which can be motivated by the temptation of speculation. In particular borrowing to fund equity investment is allowed for many investment companies, but this can be irresponsible and potentially very disruptive. If equity prices fall the company may not be able to service its debts. Mutual funds usually have regulatory limits placed on their debts and in the case of *Sharī'a* compliant funding the Dow Jones S&P *Sharī'a Board* have agreed that the debt outstanding should not exceed one third of total capital.[108] Often when equity prices fall fund managers may want to borrow to give temporary support for the market, benefiting their investors. The challenge with such intervention is that it is impossible to predict what the long term will bring and fund managers inevitably make errors of judgement. Where fund managers dominate purchases and sales of equities, this may distort the market and imply unfair competition.

Mutual funds maintain cash reserves to finance investment opportunities, as if all assets are committed and it is necessary to sell some equity holdings to purchase others this will delay transactions. For equity investment timing is crucial, and having liquid cash assets means the fund manager can focus on purchasing opportunities rather than worrying about selling. The cash holdings will normally be augmented from dividend payments from existing investments. How much cash to hold is always a debatable point, but mainstream fund managers will attempt to negotiate a return by having the cash holding in a deposit account paying interest. Islamic banks cannot earn such returns which are based on *ribā*. However the S&P Dow Jones *Sharī'a* Board permits the holding of cash and interest bearing securities provided they do not exceed one third of total assets. They also allow the holding of receivables and cash provided they do not exceed 50% of total assets. Receivables include investment into the funds which has been agreed but not yet transferred, including from pension funds which outsource investment management.

---

[107] Derigs, Ulrich/ Marzban, Shehab, "Review and analysis of current *Sharī'a*-compliant equity screening practices," *International Journal of Islamic and Middle Eastern Finance and Management* 1, 4 (2008), 285–303.
[108] Orzano, Michael / Welling, John, *How Indexing Affects Sharī'a Compliant Investing*, S&P Dow Jones Islamic Indices, New York, 2019, 1–11.

The sector screens applied by Islamic managed funds are to ensure that investments are *Sharīʿa* compliant and are not promoting economic activities which are contrary to Islamic teaching.[109] The major exclusions for finance to be *Sharīʿa* compliant are conventional banks, pork production and distribution, breweries and distilleries, gambling and casino operations and pornographic media. Conventional banks are the most notable exclusion as their shares account for more than thirty percent of total stock market capitalisation in many of the countries comprising the Organization for Islamic Cooperation (OIC). Ironically this is a higher percentage than is found for mainstream banking in Christian majority or secular countries.

Sharīʿa compliant funds can of course invest in the equity of Islamic banks, but where a mainstream bank offers *Sharīʿa* compliant products through a so-called "Islamic window" this would not qualify the bank as acceptable for investment. Even where the *Sharīʿa* compliant financial activities are overseen by a board of religious advisors equity in the bank is still viewed as inappropriate for investors concerned with *Sharīʿa* compliance. When mainstream banks decide to convert into being Islamic banks it is only at the end of the process that the equity can be included in the portfolio of a managed fund.

The prohibition of investing in pork production and distribution is because pork is regarded as impure. Pigs eat everything, including household garbage.[110] In recent years more concerns have arisen over inadvisability of pork, arguments that convince many non-Muslims. Pigs are difficult to slaughter which raises animal welfare concerns. Excessive consumption of pork can damage human health as evidence links it to cancer and heart disease. Finally, and most persuasive of all arguments, is the evidence of pigs, including those being factory farmed, contribute significantly to global warming which brings disastrous climate change for our planet. The intensification of farming is a global concern, especially given the situation in China, the leading pork consuming and producing nation. Swine fever, which has many variants, is endemic in China and a change in diet may be the only ultimate solution.

---

109 Alotaibi, Khaled O. / Hariri, Mohammad M., "Content analysis of *Sharīʿa*-compliant investment equity funds in KSA: Does social justice matter," *International Journal of Business and Management* 15, 6 (2020), 1–15.
110 Fadzlillah, Nurrulhidayah A./ Che Man, Yaakob B./ Jamaludin, Mohammad Aizat / Ab Rahman, Suhaimi, /Al-Kahtani, Hassan A., "Ḥalāl food issues from Islamic and modern science perspectives," *2nd International Conference on Humanities, Historical and Social Sciences*, International Association of Computer Science and Information Technology Press (IACSIT), 17, Singapore 2011, 159–163.

Islamic managed funds cannot invest in alcohol production or distribution as it is considered unhealthy for both the mind and body.[111] Drunken people cannot worship properly and excessive alcohol consumption results in a loss of inhibition and anti-social behaviour. Long term alcohol dependence shortens lives as it is a major cause of liver disease. Despite police vigilance drunk driving claims many lives world-wide, but is not a significant problem in Muslim majority countries.

Investment in gambling companies is also not permissible under *Sharī'a* law.[112] For some gamblers it becomes addictive and it can cause the destruction of families. It is a particular problem for men, who may try to disguise from their wives the extent of their spending on bets. All too often children may be hungry as household debt increases. Gamblers who try to cover their losses by placing new bets to escape from debt are generally deluded. In gambling it is always the casino that wins and the punters who loose in the long term.[113] Gambling and alcohol abuse are often linked as gamblers attempt to "drown their sorrows", but such behaviour only makes matters worse.

There can be little doubt that Islamic economic and financial debate has increased awareness of sinful behaviour and its link to addiction. The pronouncements of the *Sharī'a* boards carry much weight in wider Muslim society and their influence goes well beyond investors in Islamic managed funds.[114] While respecting the principles and teachings of Islam, they have also been pragmatic in their solutions to the problems identified in Islamic economics and finance. For example as it is difficult to classify the economic activities of some companies they have been prepared to introduce the concept of primary and secondary business. Investment in supermarkets, hotels and airlines is possible, according to some, even if they sell or supply alcohol. Their primary business is as food distributors or carrying passengers in the case of airlines, activities which are acceptable under *Sharī'a* law. The secondary activity can be tolerated, as this can be regard-

---

[111] Michalak, Laurence/ Trocki, Karen, "Alcohol and Islam: an overview," *Contemporary Drug Problems* 33, 4 (2006), 523–562.
[112] Rosenthal, Franz, "Gambling in Islam," in: Rosenthal, Franz (ed.), *Man versus Society in Medieval Islam*, Leiden: Brill, 2015, 335–516.
[113] Salamon, Hussin Bin/ Ebrahimi,Mansoureh / Yusoff, Kamaruzaman, "Speculation: the Islamic perspective: A study on Al-Maisir (gambling)," *Mediterranean Journal of Social Sciences* 6, 1 (2015), 371–371.
[114] Al Agha, Samah, "Money laundering from an Islamic perspective," *Journal of Money Laundering Control* 10, 4 (2007), 406–411.

ed as the responsibility of customers and not the businesses. In other words businesses behaviour cannot absolve customers of their own actions.[115]

Managed funds have proved highly successful as vehicles for Islamic investments, especially in Saudi Arabia and the Gulf states, and to a limited extent in Malaysia. The funds accept responsibility for *Sharī'a* compliance with *Sharī'a* monitoring usually being in-house. Responsibility to investors includes information provided on *ḥaram* income.[116] This arises from treasury holdings of the companies being financed. *Sharī'a* boards accept all companies have little choice but to use the services of mainstream banks, as although Islamic banking business is growing, companies are not yet in a position to solely employ Islamic banks. If companies earn *ribā* as a result of their activities they can simply state that they don't want this to be credited to their accounts. This would solely benefit the bank. The preferred alternative is to accept the payment but advice investors in the fund that the income is not *Sharī'a* compliant. Investors can then make a charitable donation of an equivalent amount. These actions means the funds are purified with good resulting from otherwise immoral earnings.

Saudi Arabia is the global leader in terms of the amount invested in Islamic managed funds.[117] The first fund was launched by the National Commercial Bank, (NCB); the largest bank in the Kingdom, in April 1995. It was designated Al Ahli Saudi traded equity fund with its asset riyal denominated. By September 2021 the total assets under management were worth SAR 28 billion (€6.32 billion) with gains averaging ten percent per annum. The minimum investment is SAR 5,000 and the management fee is a modest 0.65 percent per annum.[118] The Saudi Arabian stock market is by far the largest in the Islamic World with the most trading and a high level of liquidity. It is regarded as well regulated with the Capital Market Authority seeking to enforce international best practice.[119]

---

115 Ghaith, Majdi Ali Mohammad, "Sharī'a – based classification for the companies listed in the capital market: a proposed vision," *Psychology and Education Journal* 57, 9 (2020), 3677–3697.
116 Yunus, Saidatolakma Mohd/ al Haneef, Sayed Sikandar / Kamaruddin, Zuraidah, "Juristic methods of purifying haram incomes: an analysis in the context of Islamic banks in Malaysia," *Al-Shajarah: Journal of the International Institute of Islamic Thought and Civilization* 22, 2 (2017), 193–213.
117 Ashraf, Dawood, "Performance evaluation of Islamic mutual funds relative to conventional funds: empirical evidence from Saudi Arabia," *International Journal of Islamic and Middle Eastern Finance and Management* 6, 2 (2013), 105–121.
118 Data from the Saudi Stock Exchange, the *Tadawul*
119 Algaeed, Abdulaziz Hamad, "Capital market development and economic growth: an ARDL approach for Saudi Arabia, 1985–2018," *Journal of Business Economics and Management* 22, 2 (2021), 388–409.

There has been no attempt to revive traditional Islamic law and examine if the *ḥisbah* has any relevance for modern capital markets. The contemporary Islamic scholars, the *"ulama"*, while respecting history, are more concerned with the present. They correctly believe that there are many career opportunities in Islamic finance. Earnings of those appointed to the *Sharī'a* boards of major Islamic financial institutions on a part time basis exceed those of full time academic staff in universities. The members of *Sharī'a* boards are part of the establishment and aim to stay clear of politics. They see dangers rather than opportunities if the status quo is disturbed. They are however open to new ideas. Women are now appointed to *Sharī'a* boards in Malaysia and this may well become common practice in Saudi Arabia and the Gulf.

Most types of fund offered across the world have *Sharī'a* complaint equivalents. There are two major issues which the *Sharī'a* boards consider, firstly whether the screening criteria correspond to those already discussed. This is not a problem in Saudi Arabia where all the listed companies are *ḥalāl*, there being no alcohol production and no pork products. The second issue is whether the financing method is acceptable from an Islamic perspective. The Islamic equity funds, for example, are structured in a way that has no equivalence in classical Islamic law. There was no concept of limited liability as with *muḍārabah* contracts, possibly the closest to limited liability agreements, all investors have to share losses as well as profits. *Sharī'a* Boards view limited liability financing and *muḍārabah* as separate structures which can exist side by side. They see no problem with the concept of limited liability, the merits of which have been examined by *Sharī'a* Boards.[120] Simply prohibiting the adoption of a method of financing because it did not exist at the time of the Prophet is regarded as narrow minded.[121] Indeed what is described as the stagnation of *fiqh* during the last century of the Ottoman Empire is attributed by many as the reason for its collapse.

Islamic equity funds account for around three quarters of the total value of *Sharī'a* compliant managed investment most of which is in shares of listed companies. This remit ensures there is liquidity to guarantee the open status of the fund. In the event of an economic shock resulting in a high demand for redemptions the fund manager can sell some of the shareholdings. This reduces the size of the fund, but ensures a degree of long term confidence is maintained.

---

[120] Hasanuzzaman, S. M., "Limited liability of shareholders: an Islamic perspective," *Islamic Studies* 28, 4 (1989), 353–361.

[121] Asad, Muhammad/ Nawaz, Hafiz Muhammad Usman / Ali, Barkat, "Limited Liability of Shareholders: Islamic Perspective (A Critical Appraisal)," *Journal of Managerial Sciences* 14 (2020), 100–108.

Popular categories of Islamic funds include those based on *ijārah* contracts. These are closed ended with the finance used to invest in leased assets. Assets must be *ḥalāl* and have usufruct, and lessees must assume ownership responsibilities. The rental amount must be fixed and agreed in advance.

Islamic commodity funds are significant in Saudi Arabia, but not elsewhere, as returns are modest, but on the other hand the risks are also very low. The *Sharī'a* board will seek assurances that the commodity is in the possession of seller, as they want to confirm that there is a real trading transaction being financed. The prices must be fixed and known to the parties. There are several alternative contracts that can be used for the trading. Often it is undertaken through a *salam* contract where the investor advances funds for purchase of a commodity with funds returned on resale.[122] A popular alternative is to structure the deal through a *murābaḥah* transaction where investor buys the good and acts as a trader. These commodity contracts may be more significant in Saudi Arabia because the Kingdom has always been a centre for trading activity and the *Sharī'a* board members have more experience of what is involved in terms of financing.

Following the example of secular managed funds, Islamic funds have different projected returns, depending on the investors' willingness to take on risk. Growth funds, for example, aim to provide investors with capital gains.[123] They are sometimes described as taking an aggressive approach, deliberately seeking out risky stock. Pharmaceutical and new software companies are typical target investments. Investment in such stock can fulfil a social purpose, especially in the case of pharmaceutical companies if new vaccines, better diagnosis or more effective treatments result which can reduce human pain and misery. Positive social welfare effects are increasingly cited as important for Islamic funds.

Investors in growth funds should take a long time horizon of at least five years to allow for the smoothing out of fluctuations. Committed funds provide investment stability and are more welcomed by companies raising capital. Churning stock for its own sake, so called day trading, is not consistent with Islamic investment principles. Speculation is explicitly condemned in the Qur'ān, as like *ribā*, any gains are an unjust reward at the expense of others. It is socially divisive and creates conflicts. As with gambling it amounts to a quest for finan-

---

[122] Muhammad, Mohd Zulkifli, / Chong, Rosita, "The contract of bay'Al-Salam and Istisna'in Islamic commercial law: A comparative analysis," *Labuan e-Journal of Muamalat and Society* (2007), 21–28.

[123] Bin Mahfouz, Saeed/ Hassan, M. Kabir, "A Comparative Study between the Investment Characteristics of Islamic and Conventional Equity Mutual Funds in Saudi Arabia," *The Journal of Investing* 21, 4 (2012), 128–143.

cial gain without any effort being made. Speculation and gambling bring the danger of addiction with one family member throwing away money while other family members become destitute. Financial markets should not be seen as dens of inequity, and it is the duty of regulators to ensure that stock markets serve a useful purpose.

Managed funds should give honest advice to investors and make recommendations that are appropriate for their financial circumstances. Although the companies may prefer to have long term committed capital older investors may prefer to have regular income though dividend distributions. Others may prefer to have some uplift through capital appreciation while at the same time earning a modest income. Most Islamic managed funds providers offer balanced funds to achieve these objectives.

Hedge funds cannot be permissible in a *Sharī'a* compliant portfolio and the attempt to structure such funds in the 1990s ended largely because of their complexity and differing views amongst the *Sharī'a* scholars which made investors reluctant to put up the funding required.[124] The aim of hedge fund investment is to influence market movements rather than diversifying and taking a portfolio approach. The fund short sells in falling markets by borrowing stock, selling, and repurchasing when price is lower before stock is returned. The borrowing means leverage is introduced, magnifying the price cycles and presenting opportunities for greater gains, but also potentially greater losses. Hedge funds often cover positions by taking futures contracts. *Sharī'a* concerns on what was proposed included the abuse of market power with focused investment. The contracts included elements of *gharar* (uncertainty), *maisīr* (gambling), *jahalah* (exploitation of ignorance)[125] and *ba'i madūm* (selling something that does not exist) in selling.

In Malaysia, which prides itself on innovation in Islamic finance, the way forward included '*arboun* a down payment to secure a put option, which is permissible under their interpretation of Islamic law.[126] Extending the structural arrangements results in higher costs, but these are passed on to the client, with the fund managers receiving higher bonuses, of which analysts and commentators are highly critical.

---

[124] Mohamad, Saadiah/ Tabatabae, Ali, "Islamic hedging: gambling or risk management?" *Islamic Law and Law of the Muslim World Paper* 08–47 (2008), 1–19.
[125] Fageh, Achmad, "Digital currency perspective of Islamic law," *Maliyah: Jurnal Hukum Bisnis Islam* 11, 1 (2021), 110–128.
[126] Siham, Omrana / Rajae, Aboulaich, "Bai al arboun: A *Sharī'a* compliant alternative to conventional call options," *International Research Journal of Finance and Economics* 115 (2013), 66–75.

More aligned with Islamic finance are the lessons from the ethical investment industry. They adopt both positive and negative screening criteria, the latter including the prohibition of *ribā* and the former issues such as sustainability.[127] Funds are independently ranked for their ethical policies and pro-active fund managers try to change company policies and steer it in an ethical direction. High levels of transparency are sought and comprehensive reporting. There is an emphasis on sound corporate governance and fair treatment of workers and suppliers.

11.6 Islamic Capital Market Instruments

There have been no attempts to establish a specifically Islamic market, even in Muslim majority countries, as if it was a parallel market it might weaken the existing market by diverting investment. In any case most of the stock traded in all markets, including those of Muslim majority and Muslim minority states, is *Sharīʿa* compliant. Most of the innovation has therefore been in market instruments, not in replacing the market as a whole.

As the last section discussed, it is legitimate to trade *Sharīʿa* compliant stock. In stock markets bonds are also traded as if share prices are falling, investors may increase their bond holdings with the bond market regarded as a safe haven. The return on bonds represents interest however, which rules out faithful Muslims investing in such instruments. This results in Muslim investors not being able to build liquidity in order to protect themselves when stock prices are volatile or declining.

The introduction of *ṣukūk* Islamic securities is seen as the answer to this problem by creating a financial instrument which had many of the attributes of bonds, especially the ability to trade.[128] *Ṣukūk* are however *Sharīʿa* compliant as they do not yield interest based returns.[129] Rather the returns come from rents and profit sharing. This cannot be simply a renaming exercise, which would be misleading and would never get approval from a *Shariah* board. The difference from *ribā* based securities has to be substantive, with *ṣukūk* representing a com-

---

[127] Nainggolan, Yunieta / How, Janice / Verhoeven, Peter, "Ethical screening and financial performance: The case of Islamic equity funds," *Journal of Business Ethics* 137, 1 (2016), 83–99.
[128] Ahmad, Nursilah/ Daud, Siti Nurazira Mohd / Kefeli, Zurina, "Economic forces and the sukuk market," *Procedia-Social and Behavioral Sciences* 65 (2012), 127–133.
[129] Wilson, Rodney, "Overview of the sukuk market," in: Nathif A. Adam / Abdulakder Thomas (eds.), *Islamic Bonds: Your Guide to Issuing, Structuring and Investing in Sukuk*, London: Euromoney Books, 2004, 6–7.

pletely different asset class. As *ṣukūk* should serve a socially useful purpose the activities for which their finance is used really matter, while with bonds the focus is simply the returns compared with other bonds in the market, with no or little interest by investors in where or how the financing is to be used.

The structuring of *ṣukūk* involved using the contractual agreements already approved by *Shariah* boards for Islamic banking products. These were then securitized so that they could be traded in the same manner as bonds. For example a *Sharī'a* compliant *ijārah* leasing contract could be securitized enabling investors to buy into a future income stream from rental payments. Apart from the rental income investors had a right to sell some or all of their *ijārah* securitises during any working day at a price determined by market buyers and sellers. In other words the investors owned liquid assets that could be converted into cash whenever the need arose.

A company wanting to raise capital without the issuance of stock, which would dilute the value of the equity, could securitize some of its assets. Investors could then be invited to buy into the securitized assets, acquiring them for a time limited period, usually from three to five years in the case of an *ijārah ṣukūk*.[130] At the end of the lease agreement the company agrees to purchase the asset back at the same price as the investors paid for the initial issuance. For the investors the return is that of the rental. The investors do not benefit from a capital gain, but neither will they suffer losses unless the company defaulted on the rental payment or the repurchase agreement. The secondary market valuation of the *ṣukūk* will largely depend on the perceived trust in the company to meet its contractual obligations. Therefore in financing terms the *ṣukūk* has similar characteristics to a bond, but in legal terms, under national, secular as well as Islamic law, the issuance agreement is quite different.[131] Rather than being providers of a three to five year loan, the investors acquire a real asset which they own for the duration of the agreement. There has to be a legal sale and repurchase otherwise the agreement is not valid either under secular or Islamic law.

Critics of Islamic finance are skeptical about the merits of *ijārah* contracts. Their quibble about such agreements is that they stress form rather than subsistence. However the contracts have to be seen in a wider context as there are substantial benefits in terms of the resultant transparency of the financial data and how the funding is used. Usually Special Purpose Vehicles (SPVs) are incorporat-

---

[130] Hussin, Mohd Yahya Mohd /Muhammad, Fidlizan / Awang, Salwa Amirah, "Development of *sukuk ijarah* in Malaysia," *Journal of Islamic Economics, Banking and Finance* 8, 2 (2012), 91–102.
[131] Godlewski, Christophe J. / Turk-Ariss, Rima/ Weill, Laurent, "Sukuk vs. conventional bonds: A stock market perspective," *Journal of Comparative Economics* 41, 3 (2013), 745–761.

ed in the structuring with trusts created for these legal entities.[132] Separate accounts are provided for the SPV which brings a high level of financial disclosure. The rapid development of the *ṣukūk* market demonstrates the widespread confidence in this type of financial instrument. Fitch, the international rating agency, cites the value of *ṣukūk* outstanding in July 2021 as exceeding $US 754 billion, including not only corporate *ṣukūk*, but also the increasing issuance by governments representing sovereign *ṣukūk*.[133]

Five Muslim majority countries dominate the *ṣukūk* market: Malaysia, Saudi Arabia, Indonesia, UAE and Turkey. The most popular *ṣukūk* use the *ijārah* structures already described, but investors have many other choices depending on the time period for the *ṣukūk* until maturity. The major *ṣukūk* choices include *salam* certificates, a type of treasury bill which matures after 90 days. *Murābaḥah ṣukūk* fixed mark-up short-term trading contracts are used by investors wanting short term commercial paper rather than government securities. In the Muslim World large corporates, such as the utility companies in Saudi Arabia and the Gulf, have higher credit ratings than sovereign governments of the less successful economies.

Mushārakah ṣukūk are long term investments, often for periods of ten years or longer, which involves the investors and the existing company forming a new partnership company. They share in the profits generated, as well as from the proceeds from the sale of the partnership at maturity. There are several variants, one being that the original company seeking the finance buys the new company on maturity either at the same price as the asset purchase or at a higher price agreed at the time of the initial issuance. Another variant has the investors in the new company having their shares converted into equity in the original company, this structure being designated as convertible *ṣukūk*.[134]

The attraction of *ṣukūk* for investors is that if they wish to redeem their funds they can sell their holdings, provided there is liquidity in the market with plentiful buyers and sellers. This is certainly the case in Kuala Lumpur and Riyadh, but less developed markets are often illiquid. For long term project finance *istiṭnāʾ* contracts are usually less expensive as there are not the structuring costs as with *ṣukūk*. These contracts can be easily re-negotiated if the investors agree, unlike *ṣukūk* which are less flexible and subject to regulatory supervi-

---

132 Wilson, Rodney, "Innovation in the structuring of Islamic sukuk securities," *Humanomics* 24, 3 (2008), 170–181.
133 Fitch Ratings, *Global sukuk market growth to continue in 2021 and beyond*, Dubai, 2021.
134 Moghadam, Mesbahi / Reza, Gholam /Abadi, Ali Saleh / Etesami, Seyed Amir Hossin, "Feasibility Study of Designing the Banking Convertible Sukuk," *Islamic Economics Studies Bi-quarterly Journal* 7, 2 (2015), 173–209.

sion.[135] However there is no secondary market for *istiṭnā'* contracts and investors wanting to exit before the end of the contract are obliged to enter discussions with the originator.

There has, unsurprisingly, been some disquiet about the practice of returns on *ijārah ṣukūk* being benchmarked to interest rate proxies such as the London Interbank Offer Rate (LIBOR) or the Saudi Arabian equivalent (SAIBOR). Although the actual payments are rent these floating interest rate proxies reflect monetary policy and not the value of the asset being leased. For sovereign *ṣukūk* a more convincing practice would link Gross Domestic Product to the amounts paid for the financing. If the real economy was growing at a higher level, the government could afford to pay the investors more. Conversely if growth was lower, or even negative, the government could pay less. In other words the investment returns would reflect affordability with risks shared between *ṣukūk* investors and the state. For corporate *ṣukūk* payments could be linked to business profitability which would be consistent with the principle of risk sharing.

The Islamic Financial Services Board (IFSB) highlights the important distinction between asset-based *ṣukūk,* asset-backed *ṣukūk* and pass-through *ṣukūk*.[136] With asset backed ṣukūk the capital returned on ṣukūk maturity depends on asset value with investors subject to market risk. Asset-based ṣukūk are appropriate for *muḍārabah* and *mushārakah ṣukūk* where re-payment of capital cannot be guaranteed. They are suitable for *Sharī'a* compliant investment funds but there is significant exposure risk for *takāful* pools and Islamic pension funds. Furthermore these *ṣukūk* have merits for family, but not general, *takāful*. Pass through *ṣukūk* are also asset based, where the issuing entity (SPV) purchases assets from originator which are then packaged into a pool. The originator is required to provide recourse by the issuer. There is credit enhancement as the issuer guarantees repayment in the event of default by the originator. Pass-through *ṣukūk* cannot be used for *muḍārabah* or *mushārakah ṣukūk*. Risks for *ṣukūk* investors include credit risk where there is delay or default on payments/repayments by the originator. Market risk arises when asset values fall, reducing the repayment amount on maturity. Liquidity risk arises when there are no buyers in the secondary market for *ṣukūk*. *Salam ṣukūk* are illiquid until maturity. Risks for ṣukūk investors also include rate of return risk. *Ijārah ṣukūk* have variable re-

---

[135] Muhammad, Mohd Zulkifli/Chong, Rosita, "The contract of bay'Al-Salam and Istisna'in Islamic commercial law: A comparative analysis," *Labuan e-Journal of Muamalat and Society 1* (2007), 21–28.
[136] IFSB *Capital Adequacy Requirements for Sukuk, Securitisations and Real Estate Investment*, Kuala Lumpur, January 2009.

turns but variable to fixed rate swaps are possible and vice versa (*ijārah* ↔ *murābaḥah*). *Sharī'a* risk arises with *ijtihad* and the issuance of new *fatwa* results in *ṣukūk* no longer being *Sharī'a* compliant. Finally there is reputational risk with the arranger and issuer under pressure to maintain investor confidence.

12 Building on the Achievements of Islamic Economics to Shape Future Developments

The distribution of income and wealth has always been a concern for Islamic scholars, not least because market outcomes inevitably result in winners and losers. Closing down markets may damage the economy however, and replacing prices as a means of resource allocation by a command economy may be inefficient. Those who are well remunerated through a market system and own significant assets should recognise their obligations to wider society.

12.1 Islamic Social Welfare Provision

This is achieved by *zakāt* payments which are viewed as a religious obligation. *Zakāt* is an annual levy on assets, the amount due being one fortieth of their total value. The precise liability for *zakāt* has been much debated, as it represents a type of wealth tax with owner occupied residential property excluded but property which results in rental income included. Liquid assets are also liable for *zakāt*, including bank deposits and shareholdings in listed companies but not private equity. There is generally no personal or corporate liability for *ṣukūk* holdings, a *Sharī'a* compliant type of bond, but there could be a liability for conventional bond holdings, even though these are regarded as illegitimate assets as they yield interest, which can be classified as income from *ribā* and therefore condemned.

Proceeds from *zakāt* are allocated to the poor and needy, but there is inevitably debate about the criteria which should be applied to determine the beneficiaries.[137] Should *zakāt* be given to the old and vulnerable who suffer ill health or should the priority be to spend on education for the young? Is the aim of *zakāt* to lift the poor out of poverty and promote sustainable employment or should it

---

[137] Ahmad, Raja Adzrin Raja/ Othman, Ahmad Marzuki Amiruddin / Salleh, Muhammad Sufiyudin, "Assessing the satisfaction level of *zakat* recipients towards *zakat* management," *Procedia Economics and Finance* 31, 15 (2015), 140–151.

simply be allocated for recurrent purchases of foodstuffs? Should governments administer *zakāt* collection and distribution or is it preferable if this is undertaken by Islamic charitable foundations? If the latter, can *zakāt* payments be offset against income or corporate taxes?

As *zakāt* administration is usually undertaken at national level it is regarded as being within the sphere of macroeconomics. This contrasts with the case of *waqf*, a religious microeconomic institution established to administer the assets of a mosque, including land and other buildings on the site.[138] Legally *waqf* are a type of trust, often established by the head of a wealthy family which may be designated with the family name. If they are awarded charitable status subsequently *waqf* can obtain tax credits on donations and tax exemptions on income. The tax relief applies to all charitable activities, but the founders of the *waqf* cannot gain financially from the *trust* as it is not a business. In addition to funding the building and renovation of mosques *waqf* often fund education for those worshipping at the mosque or their families.

Zakāt and *waqf* revenues are significant sources of income in Muslim societies, but they are not substitutes for taxation which finances a wide range of secular activities. As with other religions amongst Muslims there are different views on how large the public sector should be relative to the private sector. This is considered to be beyond the remit of Islamic teaching, and although individual *imāms* may have personal views, those of their congregations may differ. This also applies to taxation and government expenditure policy with debates over the desirability of progressive income taxes or the merits of direct versus indirect taxes matters for the secular domain. There is no religious debate about the proportions of government spending allocated to defence, health, education and infrastructure.

12.2 Islam and Economic Policy

In contrast to the relative silence on fiscal policy, Islamic economists have taken an active interest in monetary policy, largely because of the prohibition of *ribā* in the Qurʿān, which many believe applies to all interest transactions.[139] The Islam-

---

[138] Hassan, Norizan / Abdul-Rahman, Aisyah / Yazid, Zaleha, "Developing a new framework of *waqf* management," *International Journal of Academic Research in Business and Social Sciences* 8, 2 (2018), 287–305.
[139] Ahmad, Abu Umar Faruq / Hassan, M. Kabir, "*Riba* and Islamic banking," *Journal of Islamic Economics, Banking and Finance* 3, 1 (2007), 1–33.

ic banking industry has taken-off during the last half century with savers rewarded by profit shares rather than interest and those being financed paying markups or rent.[140] This alternative type of banking has attracted many clients from the Muslim community, and is viewed as safe as Islamic banks are subject to the same regulation as interest based banks and meet Basel capital adequacy and liquidity requirements.

Not surprisingly there are concerns amongst Islamic economists about monetary policy which involves setting interest rates to achieve inflationary targets.[141] If interest rates rise because monetary policy is tightened this implies those being financed often have to pay more, but savers may obtain a windfall reward. Manipulating interest rates because of macroeconomic targets is seen as unjust to those who have payments obligations. Having fixed interest contracts often does not help, not least because fixed interest financing is often more expensive than variable rate contracts. Despite these concerns Islamic economists have so far failed to suggest a viable alternative to current monetary practices. There is much further research needed if Islamic teaching is to say more concerning economic policy.[142]

Conclusion: The Ways Forward

What are the findings from this exploration of the concept of economy in Islam? Looking back and re-visiting the relevant *sūra* in the *Qurʾān* and being acquainted with the *Hadīth* is clearly an appropriate starting point. It is not the finish however, as Islamic economics today is quite different from what it was fifty years ago, and even more removed from what it was at the time of the Prophet. The subject can be seen as inherently dynamic rather than static, evolving as mainstream economics advances. It is more than a field of historical enquiry, although the historical economic experiences of Muslim society, states and empires deserve more attention.

In terms of methodology the approaches of writers such as Muhammad Umer Chapra have been discussed, notably his critique of classical and neo-classical, essentially secular, economics. Contemporary economics is branching out on many fronts, with important advances in behavioural economics, anthropo-

---

[140] Iqbal, Munawar / Molyneux, Philip, *Thirty Years of Islamic Banking: History, Performance and Prospects*. London: Palgrave Macmillan, 2016.
[141] Khan, Mohsin S. / Mirakhor, Abbas, "The financial system and monetary policy in an Islamic economy," *Journal of King Abdulaziz University: Islamic Economics* 1, 1 (1989), 39–57.
[142] Wilson, Rodney, *Islam and Economic Policy*, Edinburgh: Edinburgh University Press, 2015.

logical economics and institutional economics, as well as at the interface of law and economics. It would be good to see the younger generations of researchers in Islamic economics engage with these new sub-disciplines.

Most research in economics and finance today is evidence based, often involving mathematical modelling and statistical testing to determine the relationship between economic variables. In addition to quantitative analysis, qualitative studies are becoming increasingly useful. Given the enormous growth of Islamic banking and other Islamic financial intermediaries, huge quantities of data have been accumulating. Researchers are already using these data sets but the scope for evidence based investigations is getting ever greater. Islamic accountancy has emerged as a separate sub-discipline, and this work is potentially of great value to those engaged in Islamic economics and finance.

Topics such as the implications of the prohibition of *ribā*, the regulation of markets and *Sharīʿa* governance have been researched intensely, but new datasets could make the effort more extensive. Not surprisingly work is already ongoing on the economics of pandemics. Also receiving attention are sustainable development issues related to adverse climatic effects of using fossil fuels as an energy source. As high income Muslim majority states use a substantial amount of oil and gas for the production of electricity, the economic costs of such policy priorities merits investigation.

Prospects for Islamic economics are promising given its moral and ethical agenda. Secular economics has a useful tool-kit, but it does not arouse the same passions as Islamic economics. The practitioners in Islamic economics feel they are involved with an endeavour which is very worthwhile. This together with sympathetic funding institutions undoubtedly helps research. Furthermore although the media is too often critical of Muslim majority countries the reality is rather different, at least as far as economic activity is concerned.

There are no designated Islamic economies and it is doubtful if there ever will be. However where Muslims feel uncomfortable with economic practices and regard them as incompatible with Islamic teaching, changes have occurred, as with the development of Islamic banking, *takāful* and *Sharīʿa* compliant investment management. If required new institution building can be extended into other areas of economic activity as part of an open agenda.

Bibliography

Abduh, Muhamad / Azmi Omar, Mohd / Duasa, Jarita, "The impact of crisis and macroeconomic variables towards Islamic banking deposits," *American Journal of Applied Sciences* 8, 12 (2011), 1413–1418.

Abdullah, Mohammad, "Analysing the moral aspect of qard: a shariah perspective," *International Journal of Islamic and Middle Eastern Finance and Management* 8, 2 (2015), 171–184.

Ahmad, Abu Umar Faruq / Hassan, M. Kabir, "Ribā and Islamic banking," *Journal of Islamic Economics, Banking and Finance* 3, 1 (2007), 1–33.

Ahmad, Nursilah / Daud, Siti Nurazira Mohd / Kefeli, Zurina, "Economic forces and the ṣukūk market," *Procedia-Social and Behavioral Sciences* 65 (2012), 127–133.

Ahmad, Raja Adzrin Raja / Othman, Ahmad Marzuki Amiruddin / Salleh, Muhammad Sufiyudin, "Assessing the satisfaction level of zakāt recipients towards zakāt management," *Procedia Economics and Finance* 31, 15 (2015), 140–151.

Ahmad, Saiyad Nizamuddin, "Twelver Šīʿī Ḥadit: from tradition to contemporary evaluations," *Oriente Moderno* 21, 1 (2002), 125–145.

Ahmed, Zahid Shahab / Akbarzadeh, Shahram, "Sectarianism and the Organisation of Islamic Cooperation (OIC)," *Territory, Politics, Governance* 9, 1 (2021), 76–93.

Akhtar, Beenish / Akhter, Waheed /Shahbaz, Muhammad, "Determinants of deposits in conventional and Islamic banking: a case of an emerging economy," *International Journal of Emerging Markets* 12, 2 (2017), 296–309.

Al Agha, Samah, "Money laundering from an Islamic perspective," *Journal of Money Laundering Control* 10, 4 (2007), 406–411.

Al Arif, M. Nur Rianto, "Monopoly and Ikhtikar in Islamic Economics," *Shirkah: Journal of Economics and Business* 1, (2016), 299–310.

Al Noumani, Dalal / Al Mutairi, Fawaz / Machado, Julian, "Kuwait Finance House," *International Journal of Accounting & Finance in Asia Pasific* 2, (2019), 1–4.

Algaeed, Abdulaziz Hamad, "Capital market development and economic growth: an ARDL approach for Saudi Arabia, 1985–2018," *Journal of Business Economics and Management* 22, 2 (2021), 388–409.

Ali, M. Mahbubi / Hassan, Rusni / Hasan, Shabana M., "An exploratory study of Sharīʿa issues in the application of Tabarruʾfor takāful," *Global Review of Islamic Economics and Business* 1, 3 (2015), 164–174.

Alotaibi, Khaled O. / Hariri, Mohammad M., "Content analysis of Sharīʿa-compliant investment equity funds in KSA: Does social justice matter," *International Journal of Business and Management* 15, 6 (2020), 1–15.

Al-Rikabi, Jaffar, "Baqir al-Sadr and the Islamic State: A Theory for 'Islamic Democracy'," *Journal of Shiʾa Islamic Studies* 5, (2012), 249–275.

Al-Tamimi, Hussein A. Hassan / Al-Amiri, Abdullah, "Analysing service quality in the UAE Islamic banks," *Journal of Financial Services Marketing* 8, 2 (2003), 119–132.

Anwar, Muhammad, "Islamic banking in Iran and Pakistan: a comparative study," *The Pakistan Development Review* 31, 4 (1992), 1089–1097.

Arif, Muhammad, "Toward a definition of Islamic economics: some scientific considerations," *Journal of King Abdulaziz University: Islamic Economics* 2, 2 (1985), 79–93.

Asad, Muhammad/ Nawaz, Hafiz Muhammad Usman / Ali, Barkat, "Limited Liability of Shareholders: Islamic Perspective (A Critical Appraisal)," *Journal of Managerial Sciences* 14 (2020), 100–108.

Ashraf, Dawood, "Performance evaluation of Islamic mutual funds relative to conventional funds: empirical evidence from Saudi Arabia," *International Journal of Islamic and Middle Eastern Finance and Management* 6, 2 (2013), 105–121.

Ashraf, S. Husain / Giashi, Ali Alizadeh, "Islamic banking in Iran: Progress and challenges," *Kuwait Chapter of Arabian Journal of Business and Management Review* 33, 830 (2011), 1–28.

Aziz, Talib M., "The role of Muhammad Baqir al-Sadr in Shi'i political activism in Iraq from 1958 to 1980," *International Journal of Middle East Studies* 25, (1993), 207–222.

Aziz, Tareq M., "An Islamic perspective of political economy: The views of (late) Muhammad Baqir al-Sadr," *Al-Tawhid Islamic Journal* 10, (1993).

Banisadr, Abolhassan, "Iran at the crossroads," *New Perspectives Quarterly* 27, 1 (2010), 45–49.

Becker, Sascha O. / Rubin, Jared / Woessmann, Ludger, "Religion in economic history: A survey," *The Handbook of Historical Economics* (2021), 585–639.

Belabes, Abderrazak / Belouafi, Ahmed / Daoudi, Mohamed, "Designing Islamic Finance Programmes in a Competitive Educational Space: The Islamic Economics Institute Experiment," *Procedia-Social and Behavioral Sciences 191* (2015), 639–643.

Bensaid, Benaouda / Grine, Fadila, / Nor, Mohd Roslan Mohd / Yusoff, M. Y. Z. M., "Enduring financial debt: An Islamic perspective," *Middle-East Journal of Scientific Research* 13, (2013), 162–170.

Billah, Mohd Ma'Sum, "Islamic Leasing Leading to Ownership (Al-Ijārah Tantahi Bi Al-Tamleek)," In: Islamic Financial Products, Cham: Palgrave Macmillan, 2019, 243–254.

Bin Mahfouz, Saeed/ Hassan, M. Kabir, "A Comparative Study between the Investment Characteristics of Islamic and Conventional Equity Mutual Funds in Saudi Arabia," *The Journal of Investing* 21, 4 (2012), 128–143.

Boulakia, Jean David C, "Ibn Khaldūn: a fourteenth-century economist," *Journal of Political Economy* 79, 5 (1971), 1105–1118.

Calder, Ryan, "God's Technicians: Religious Jurists and the Usury Ban in Judaism, Christianity, and Islam," *European Journal of Sociology/Archives Européennes de Sociologie* 57, 2 (2016), 207–257.

Chiswick, Carmel Ullman, *Judaism in Transition: How Economic Choices Shape Religious Tradition*, Stanford University Press, 2014.

Cattelan, Valentino, "From the concept of haqq to the prohibitions of ribā, gharar and maysir in Islamic finance," *International Journal of Monetary Economics and Finance* 2, 3–4 (2009), 384–397.

Chapra, M. Umer, "Ibn Khaldūn's theory of development: does it help explain the low performance of the present-day Muslim world?" *The Journal of Socio-Economics* 37, 2 (2008), 836–863.

Chapra, M. Umer, "Is it necessary to have Islamic economics?" *The Journal of Socio-Economics* 29, 1 (2000), 21–37.

Chapra, M. Umer, *Morality and Justice in Islamic Economics and Finance*, Cheltenham: Edward Elgar Publishing, 2014.

Charfeddine, Lanouar / Najah, Ahlem / Teulon, Frédéric, "Socially responsible investing and Islamic funds: New perspectives for portfolio allocation," *Research in International Business and Finance* 36 (2016), 351–361.

Choudhury, Masudul Alam, "Islamic economics as a social science," *International Journal of Social Economics* 17, 6 (1990), 35–69.

Choudhury, Masudul Alam, "Principles of Islamic economics," *Middle Eastern Studies* 19, 1 (1983), 93–103.

De Belder, Richard T. / Khan, Mansoor Hassan, "The changing face of Islamic banking," *International Finance Law Review* 12 (1993), 23–29.

Derigs, Ulrich/ Marzban, Shehab, "Review and analysis of current Sharīʿa-compliant equity screening practices," *International Journal of Islamic and Middle Eastern Finance and Management* 1, 4 (2008), 285–303.

Diab, Muhammad, "The Arab common market," *Journal of Common Market Stud.* 4 (1965), 238–246.

Doniyorov, Alisher Khudoyberdiyevich /Karimov, Nodir Rakhmonqulovich, "An Incomparable Book of a Great Scholar," *Bulletin Social-Economic and Humanitarian Research* 6 (2020), 63–71.

Ead, Hamed A. and Nada H. Eid, "Between Ibn Khaldūn and Adam Smith (Fathers of Economics)," *IOSR Journal of Business and Management* 3 (2014), 54–56.

El-Ashker, Ahmed / Wilson, Rodney, *Islamic Economics: A Short History*, Leiden: Brill, 2006.

El-Gamal, Mahmoud A., "An economic explication of the prohibition of Ribā in classical Islamic jurisprudence," *Proceedings of the Third Harvard University Forum on Islamic Finance*, 31–44, Cambridge: Center for Middle Eastern Studies, Harvard University, 2000.

Elsanousi, Mohamed/ Visotzky, Burton L. / Roberts, Bob, *Love your neighbour: Islam, Judaism and Christianity come together over COVID-19*, Western Michigan University, 2020.

Fadzlillah, Nurrulhidayah A./ Che Man, Yaakob B./ Jamaludin, Mohammad Aizat / Ab Rahman, Suhaimi, /Al-Kahtani, Hassan A., "Ḥalāl food issues from Islamic and modern science perspectives," *2nd International Conference on Humanities, Historical and Social Sciences*, International Association of Computer Science and Information Technology Press (IACSIT), 17, Singapore 2011, 159–163.

Fageh, Achmad, "Digital currency perspective of Islamic law," *Maliyah: Jurnal Hukum Bisnis Islam* 11, 1 (2021), 110–128.

Farook, Sayd Zubair / Farooq, Mohammad Omar, *Sharīʿa governance for Islamic finance: Challenges and pragmatic solutions*, Available at SSRN 1813483 (2011).

Farooq, Mohammad Omar, "The ribā-interest equation and Islam: reexamination of the traditional arguments," *Global Journal of Finance and Economics* 6, 2 (2009), 99–111.

Fildis, Ayse Tekdal, "Roots of Alawite-Sunni Rivalry in Syria," *Middle East Policy* 19, 2 (2012), 148–156.

Fitch Ratings, *Global ṣukūk market growth to continue in 2021 and beyond*, Dubai, 2021.

Furqani, Hafas. "Consumption and morality: Principles and behavioral framework in Islamic economics," *Journal of King Abdulaziz University: Islamic Economics* 30 (2017) 89–102.

Furqani, Hafas, "Consumption and morality: Principles and behavioral framework in Islamic economics," *Journal of King Abdulaziz University: Islamic Economics* 30 (2017), 89–102.

Ghaith, Majdi Ali Mohammad, "Sharīʿa – based classification for the companies listed in the capital market: a proposed vision," *Psychology and Education Journal* 57, 9 (2020), 3677–3697.

Godlewski, Christophe J. / Turk-Ariss, Rima/ Weill, Laurent, "Ṣukūk vs. conventional bonds: A stock market perspective," *Journal of Comparative Economics* 41, 3 (2013), 745–761.

Hamid, Mohamad Abdul, "Sharīʿa compliance of wakalah concept in Takāful operation: A case study of a Takāful operation in Malaysia," *Tazkia Islamic Finance and Business Review* 8, 2 (2014), 1–26.

Haneef, Mohamed Aslam, "Islam, the Islamic worldview, and Islamic economics," *International Islamic University Malaysia Journal of Economics and Management* 5, 1 (1997), 39–65.

Haron, Abdullah, "Integrating Islamic finance to the global financial system: the role of the Islamic Financial Services Board (IFSB)," *Money and Economy* 7, 1 (2012), 67–85.

Hasan, Zubair, "Sustainable development from an Islamic perspective: meaning, implications, and policy concerns," *Journal of King Abdulaziz University: Islamic Economics* 19, 1 (2006), 3–18.

Hasan, Zubair, "Risk sharing versus risk transfer in Islamic Finance: a critical appraisal," International Sharīʿa Research Academy (ISRA), *International Journal of Islamic Finance* 7, 1 (2015), 7–24.

Hasanuzzaman, S. M., "Limited liability of shareholders: an Islamic perspective," *Islamic Studies* 28, 4 (1989), 353–361.

Hassan, A. B. U. L., "Islamic economics and the environment: Material flow analysis in society-nature interrelationships," *Journal of King Abdulaziz University: Islamic Economics* 18, 1 (2005), 15–31.

Hassan, Norizan / Abdul-Rahman, Aisyah / Yazid, Zaleha, "Developing a new framework of waqf management," *International Journal of Academic Research in Business and Social Sciences* 8, 2 (2018), 287–305.

Hayat, Raphie / Den Butter, Frank / Kock, Udo, "Ḥalāl certification for financial products: A transaction cost perspective," *Journal of Business Ethics* 117, 3 (2013), 601–613.

Hernandez, Diego / Vadlamannati, Krishna Chaitanya, "Politics of religiously motivated lending: An empirical analysis of aid allocation by the Islamic Development Bank," *Journal of Comparative Economics* 45, 4 (2017), 910–929.

Howson, Susan, "The origins of Lionel Robbins's essay on the nature and significance of economic science," *History of Political Economy* 36, 3 (2004), 413–443.

Hussain, Mher Mushtaq / Pasha, Ahmad Tisman, "Conceptual and operational differences between general takāful and conventional insurance," *Australian Journal of Business and Management Research* 1, 8 (2011), 23–28.

Hussin, Mohd Yahya Mohd /Muhammad, Fidlizan / Awang, Salwa Amirah, "Development of ṣukūk ijārah in Malaysia," *Journal of Islamic Economics, Banking and Finance* 8, 2 (2012), 91–102.

IFSB, *Capital Adequacy Requirements for Ṣukūk, Securitisations and Real Estate Investment*, Kuala Lumpur, January 2009.

Ilmy, Rizky Maidan /Setiawan, Iwan, "The Concept of Production, Distribution, and Consumption in Islamic Economics," *Review of Islamic Economics and Finance (RIEF)* 2, 1 (2019), 41–46.

Iqbal, Munawar / Molyneux, Philip, *Thirty Years of Islamic Banking: History, Performance and Prospects*, London: Palgrave Macmillan, 2016.

Islahi, Abdul Azim, "Market Mechanism in Islam: A Historical Perspective," *International Journal of Economics, Management and Accounting* 3, 2 (1995), 1–13.

Islahi, Abdul Azim, *History of Islamic Economic Thought: Contributions of Muslim Scholars to Economic Thought and Analysis*, Cheltenham: Edward Elgar Publishing, 2014.

Ismal, Rifki, "Assessing moral hazard problem in Murābaḥah financing," *Journal of Islamic Economics, Banking and Finance* 5, 2 (2009), 101–112.

Karbhari, Yusuf / Alam, M. Kausar /Rahman, M. Mizanur, "Relevance of the application of institutional theory in Shariah governance of Islamic banks," *PSU Research Review* (2020), 1–15.
Khalil, Mohammad Hassan, "Ibn Taimīyah on reason and revelation in ethics," *Journal of Islamic Philosophy* 2, 1 (2006), 103–132.
Khan, Ajaz Ahmad / Thaut, Laura, "An Islamic perspective on fair trade," *United Kingdom: Islamic Relief* (2008), 1–13.
Khan, Janas / Dad, Karim, "Importance of Commerce and Trade in the Light of the Holy Qur'ān and Sunnah," *Gomal University Journal of Research*, 30, 1 (2014), 131–135.
Khan, M. Fahim, "Fiqh foundations of the theory of Islamic economics: a survey of selected contemporary writings on economics relevant subjects of fiqh," *Theoretical foundations of Islamic economics* 3 (2002), 59–85.
Khan, Mohsin S. / Mirakhor, Abbas, "The financial system and monetary policy in an Islamic economy," *Journal of King Abdulaziz University: Islamic Economics* 1, 1 (1989), 39–57.
Khan, Muhammad Akram, "Methodology of Islamic economics," *International Journal of Economics, Management and Accounting* 1, 1 (1987).
Kontorovich, Eugene, "The Arab League boycott and WTO accession: can foreign policy excuse discriminatory sanctions?," *Chicago Journal of International Law*, 4 (2003), 283.
Krokus, Christian S, "Catholic Saints and Scholars: Nostra Aetate and Islam," Nostra Aetate, Non-Christian Religions, and Interfaith Relations, 115–137, Cham: Palgrave Macmillan, 2021.
Kuran, Timur, "The discontents of Islamic economic morality," *The American Economic Review* 86, 2 (1996), 438–442.
Kuran, Timur, *Islam and Mammon: The Economic Predicaments of Islamism*, Princeton University Press, 2004.
Lateef, Adeyemo Wale/ Abdurrazzaq, Alawiye Abdulmumin/ Abdul Shukor, Syahirah/ Ahmad Tajudin, Amalina, "Maqasid Al-Sharī'a in Ijārah (Leasing) Contract of Islamic Banking System," *Journal of Islamic Finance* 6, 2 (2017), 38–44.
Mahdī, Ali Akbar, "The student movement in the Islamic Republic of Iran," *Journal of Iranian Research and Analysis* 15, 2 (1999), 5–32.
Matthews, Robin/ Tlemsani, Issam / Siddiqui, Aftab, "Recent developments in the market for Islamic mortgages: Theory and practice," *Review of Islamic Economics* 14 (2003), 49–68.
Mayer, Ann Elizabeth, "Islamic Banking and Credit Polices in the Sadat Era: The Social Origins of Islamic Banking in Egypt," *Arab Law Quarterly* 1, 1 (1985), 32–50.
Maysami, Ramin Cooper/ Kwon, W. Jean, "An Analysis of Islamic Takāful Insurance," *Journal of Insurance Regulation* 18, 1 (1999), 109–133.
Moghadam, Mesbahi / Reza, Gholam /Abadi, Ali Saleh / Etesami, Seyed Amir Hossin, "Feasibility Study of Designing the Banking Convertible Ṣukūk," *Islamic Economics Studies Bi-quarterly Journal* 7, 2 (2015), 173–209.
Orzano, Michael / Welling, John, *How Indexing Affects Sharī'a Compliant Investing*, S&P Dow Jones Islamic Indices, New York, 2019, 1–11.
Michalak, Laurence/ Trocki, Karen, "Alcohol and Islam: an overview," *Contemporary Drug Problems* 33, 4 (2006), 523–562.

Mihajat, Muhammad Iman Sastra, "Contemporary practice of Ribā, Gharar and Maysir in Islamic banking and finance," *International Journal of Islamic Management and Business* 2, (2016), 1–19.

Mohamad, Saadiah/ Tabatabae, Ali, "Islamic hedging: gambling or risk management?" *Islamic Law and Law of the Muslim World Paper* 08–47 (2008), 1–19.

Mohammad, Fida, "Ibn Khaldūn's theory of social change: a comparison with Hegel, Marx and Durkheim," *American Journal of Islamic Social Sciences* 15, 2 (1998), 25–39.

Muhammad, Abid Mahmood, "Critical analysis of some of the major internal hindrance factors in the application of Mushārakah financing by the Islamic banks," *International Journal of Education and Research* 2, 9 (2014), 125–142.

Muhammad, Mohd Zulkifli, / Chong, Rosita, "The contract of bay'Al-Salam and Istisna'in Islamic commercial law: A comparative analysis," *Labuan e-Journal of Muamalat and Society* 1 (2007), 21–28.

Muqorobin, Masyhudi, "Journey of Islamic economics in the modern world," *Proceedings of The Seventh International Conference on Islamic Economics*, 385–404, 2008.

Nagaoka, Shinsuke, "Critical overview of the history of Islamic economics: formation, transformation, and new horizons," *Asian and African Area Studies* 11, 2 (2012), 114–136.

Nainggolan, Yunieta/ How,Janice / Verhoeven, Peter, "Ethical screening and financial performance: The case of Islamic equity funds," *Journal of Business Ethics* 137, 1 (2016), 83–99.

Naqvi, Syed Nawab Haider (ed.), *Islam, Economics, and Society (RLE Politics of Islam)*, London: Routledge, 2013.

Nawaz, Tasawar / Haniffa, Roszaini / Hudaib, Mohammad, "On intellectual capital efficiency and Sharī'a governance in Islamic banking business model," *International Journal of Finance & Economics* 26, 3 (2021), 3770–3787.

Norbaya, Siti,/Abd Hadi Abd Rahman, Muhammad/ Che Yahya, Norliza/ Md Rasid, NorFarah, "Bai Bithaman Ajil (BBA) and Mushārakah Mutanaqisah (MM): Comparative Analysis," *Advances in Business Research Journal* 6, 2 (2020), 19–29.

Nu'Man, Ruqiyyah, / Ali, S. Nazim, "Islamic economics and finance education: consensus on reform," *Journal of Faculty of Islamic Studies-Hamad Bin Khalifa University* (2016), 76–97.

Palmer, Monte, "The United Arab Republic: an assessment of its failure," *Middle East Journal* 20, 1 (1966), 50–67.

Presley, John R. / Sessions, John G., "Islamic economics: the emergence of a new paradigm," *The Economic Journal* 104, 424 (1994), 584–596.

Read, Daniel, "Experienced utility: utility theory from Jeremy Bentham to Daniel Kahneman," *Thinking and Reasoning* 13, 1 (2007), 45–61.

Redzuan, Hendon / Abdul Rahman, Zuriah / Aidid, S. S. S. H., "Economic determinants of family takāful consumption: Evidence from Malaysia," *International Review of Business Research Papers* 5, 5 (2009), 193–211.

Rehman, Asma Abdul / Masood, Omar, "Why do customers patronize Islamic banks? A case study of Pakistan," *Qualitative Research in Financial Markets* 4, 2/3 (2012), 130–141.

Rosenthal, Franz, "Gambling in Islam,"in: Ibd., *Man versus Society in Medieval Islam*, Leiden: Brill, 2015, 335–516.

Sairally, Beebee Salma, "Murābaḥah financing: Some controversial issues," *Review of Islamic Economics* (2002), 73–86.
Salamon, Hussin Bin/ Ebrahimi,Mansoureh / Yusoff, Kamaruzaman, "Speculation: the Islamic perspective: A study on Al-Maisir (gambling)," *Mediterranean Journal of Social Sciences* 6, 1 (2015), 371–371.
Salim, Suna / Abdullah, Syahrul Faizaz / Ahmad, Kamarudin, "Wilayat Al-Hisba; a means to achieve justice and maintain high ethical standards in societies," *Mediterranean Journal of Social Sciences* 6, 4 S2 (2015), 201–206.
Samiullah, Muhammad, "Prohibition of ribā (interest) and insurance in the light of Islam," *Islamic Studies* 21, 2 (1982), 53–76.
Sarea, Adel Mohammed / Hanefah, Mustafa Mohd, "The need of accounting standards for Islamic financial institutions: evidence from AAOIFI," *Journal of Islamic Accounting and Business Research* 4, 1 (2013), 64–76.
Setiawan, Romi Adetio, "The relevance of Ibn Taimīyah economics in addressing poverty and income distribution," *Madania: Jurnal Kal Kajian Keislaman*, 20, 1 (2016), 13–22.
Shavit, Uriya, "A Fatwa and Its Dialectics: Contextualizing the Permissibility of Mortgages in Stockholm," *Journal of Muslims in Europe* 8, 3 (2019), 335–358.
Siddiqi, M. Nejatullah, "Sharī'a, economics and the progress of Islamic finance: the role of Sharī'a experts," Concept Paper presented at Pre-Forum Workshop on Select Ethical and Methodological Issues in Shari'a-Compliant Finance, Cambridge, Massachusetts, USA, 2006.
Siham, Omrana/ Rajae, Aboulaich, "Bai al arboun: A Sharī'a compliant alternative to conventional call options," *International Research Journal of Finance and Economics* 115 (2013), 66–75.
Spengler, Joseph J., "Economic thought of Islam: Ibn Khaldūn," *Comparative Studies in Society and History* 6, 3 (1964), 268–306.
Tameme, Mohammed /Asutay, Mehmet, "An empirical inquiry into marketing Islamic mortgages in the UK," *International Journal of Bank Marketing* (2012), 49–68.
Usman, Abur Hamdi /Ismail, Abu Zaki / Soroni, Mohd Khafidz / Wazir, Rosni, "Rise and Fall of Development: How does Hadīth View the Economic System?" *Asian Social Science* 11, 27 (2015), 168–174.
Wilson, Rodney, "Comparative religious thought on economic behaviour and financial transactions", *Association of Christian Economists Journal* 23, (1997), 1–10.
Wilson, Rodney, *Islam and Economic Policy*, Edinburgh: Edinburgh University Press, 2015.
Wilson, Rodney, "Innovation in the structuring of Islamic ṣukūk securities," *Humanomics* 24, 3 (2008), 170–181.
Wilson, Rodney, "Islam and business," *Thunderbird International Business Review* 48, 1 (2006), 109–123.
Wilson, Rodney, "Overview of the ṣukūk market," Adam, Nathif A. / Thomas, Abdulakder (eds.), *Islamic Bonds: Your Guide to Issuing, Structuring and Investing in Ṣukūk*, London: Euromoney Books (2004), 6–7.
Wilson, Rodney, "Economics and morality from an Islamic perspective", Hassan, M. Kabir / Lewis, Mervyn K. (eds.), *Handbook on Islam and Economic Life*, Cheltenham: Edward Elgar (2014), 268–282.
Wilson, Rodney, *Economic Development in the Middle East*, 3rd edition, London and New York: Routledge (2022), 113–114.

Wilson, Rodney, *Economics, Ethics and Religion: Jewish, Christian and Muslim Economic Thought*, London: Palgrave Macmillan, 1997.

Wilson, Rodney, "The application of Islamic thought to economic policy making in a threatened world", *Journal of Islamic Economics*, 34, 2 (2021), 157–162.

Wilson, Rodney, "The contribution of Muhammad Baqir Al-Sadr to contemporary Islamic economic thought", *Journal of Islamic Studies*, 9, 1, (1998), 46–59.

Yazid, Ahmad Shukri/ Arifin,Juliana/ Hussin, Mohd Rasid/ Wan Daud, Wan Norhayate, "Determinants of family takāful (Islamic life insurance) demand: a conceptual framework for a Malaysian study," *International Journal of Business and Management* 7, 6 (2012), 115–127.

Yunus, Saidatolakma Mohd/ al Haneef, Sayed Sikandar / Kamaruddin, Zuraidah, "Juristic methods of purifying ḥaram incomes: an analysis in the context of Islamic banks in Malaysia," *Al-Shajarah: Journal of the International Institute of Islamic Thought and Civilization* 22, 2 (2017), 193–213.

Yusoff, Remali/ Wilson, Rodney, "An econometric analysis of conventional and Islamic bank deposits in Malaysia," *Review of Islamic Economics* 9, 1 (2005), 31–52.

Yusuf Saleem, Muhammad, "Methods and methodologies in fiqh and Islamic economics," Research Paper, Department of Economics Kulliyyah of Economics and Management Sciences, International Islamic University Malaysia, 1–17.

Suggestions for further reading

El-Asker, Ahmad Abdel Fattah / Wilson, Rodney, *Islamic Economics: A Short History*, Leiden: Brill, 2006.

Mirakhor, Abbas / Askari; Hossein / Iqbal, Zamir, *Introduction to Islamic Economics: Theory and Practice*, Singapore: Wiley, 2014.

Islahi, Abdul Azim, *History of Islamic Economic Thought: Contributions of Muslim Scholars to Economic Thought and Analysis*, Cheltenham: Edward Elgar, 2014.

Asutay Mehmet / Shafiullah, Jan, *A Model for Islamic Development: An Approach in Islamic Moral Economy*, Cheltenham: Edward Elgar, 2019.

Visser, Hans, *Islamic Finance: Principles and Practices*, Northampton: Edward Elgar, 2019, 3rd edition.

Hasan, Zulkfini, *Shari'ah Governance in Islamic Banks*, Edinburgh: Edinburgh University Press and Berlin: De Gruyter, 2012.

Ali, S. Nazim / Nizar, Shariq (eds), *Takaful and Islamic Cooperative Finance*, Cheltenham: Edward Elgar, 2016.

Hassan, Kabir and Mahlknecht, Michael, *Islamic Capital Markets*, Chichester: Wiley, 2015.

Hassan, Kabir, *Islamic Corporate Finance*, Oxon: Routledge, 2019.

Safari, Meysam / Ariff, Mohamed / Shamsher, *Sukuk Securities: New Ways of Debt Contracting*, Singapore: Wiley, 2014.

Christoph Böttigheimer and Wenzel M. Widenka
Epilogue

Introduction

The way of doing business is part of man's interaction with creation. In the context of the ecological crisis, the focus is not only increasingly on the economic order, but also on economic practice in the holy scriptures of all three monotheistic religions. In principle, believers are not detached from their religion in their economic actions and must act out of a sense of responsibility before God. Responsible action is characterised by an orientation towards the common good, even though many ideas of social justice have only become concrete in modern times. In this context, the prohibition of interest on money is certainly of interest, which is known both in Islam and was demanded, for example, by Martin Luther and Jewish religious scholars. This leads us to the questions that are of interest with regard to the ecological actions of believers, such as: What about the legitimacy of property? How is the pursuit of profit maximisation compatible with social obligation? Or: What are the connections between the principles of a social market economy and an Islamic economic order? The following summary gives an overview over the fundamental ideas explicated in the texts of this volume.

The Concept of Economy from a Jewish Perspective

The most striking feature about Judaism's perception of wealth is that it has a fundamentally positive approach towards it. Wealth itself is a sacred gift, it is to be accepted and appreciated as a sign of divine love, meant to ease human life. This having said it surely must be added that it crucially depends on which kind of wealth we're talking about. First of all the nature of wealth is determined by the laws of the covenant between God and his creation and who's most significant result is the giving of the *Torah*. Thus, it is a religious and sacred perspective on wealth and both the use and meaning of wealth for a society and the implementation of an "economic" idea are to be seen in the light of a sacred sphere, not a secular one. Wealth and economics are thus genuine religious questions and issues. They are meant to valorise human and social life and agency; they are not ends in themselves or ways of accumulating money or property.

As a religion that is unquestionably bound to a promised land and that finds its origins in a pastoral society, it is not surprising that "wealth" in Judaism is primarily defined as ownership of land and cattle. It is not a question of money. The land does not only belong to its human owner, but it is also a gift of God and remains in the ownership of God. The institution of the Jubilee Sabbatical Year, where the land lies fallow and all depts are cancelled is a vivid expression of a religious conception of wealth and thus economy. Here we do not find a concept of economics at all if economics is defined as a sphere distinguished from the religious area, following its own rules and regularities. A famous result of this "transcendental" treatment of economic issues is the prohibition of usury, a concept and gift Judaism gave to and shares with the two other major monotheistic religions, even if they may set a different focus and rigorousness to the issue. It is obvious that under such a sacred perception the idea of wealth (aka: money) creating even more wealth, i.e. the core principle and fundamental idea of capitalism and modern economic thought, is foreign to a Jewish idea of wealth under the regulations of the covenant. This is the perspective of the Jewish scriptures and they not only contradict with many of more modern thoughts about a just economy and the idea of ownership (e.g. the holding of slaves) but already in Biblical times the ideals of the scripture contradicted to factual everyday living conditions. Life in biblical times was normally hard and far away from the ideals of the Torah. The individual had to rely on human cooperation and the values given by the covenantal perception of shared wealth, e.g. caring for the poor. Mere self-interest would have cancelled the life-spending covenant between God and his people. Therefore, Biblical stories tell the reader about the problems of farmers and sheepherders, merchants rarely appear. Without the secular sphere of trade, wealth and economy remained questions of human-divine communication or, to put it simply, they were questions of survival. Throughout Jewish history, however, things changed. The transformation of a pastoral society into a centralised monarchy also came hand in hand with a new perception of and need for trade. Wealth suddenly was no longer a question of "Who has more sheep?" within a society that shared more or less the same living conditions, but a significant change in lifestyle and attitude towards money and property. Increasing international trade brought wealth beyond landholding and cattle to Israel. Lending money on interest became usual and the frontiers towards the long forbidden usury were easily crossed. Unequal living conditions were now at stake. With the establishment of a royal sphere apart from the sacred sphere of the covenant (of course to be thought of not as a sharp distinction but within the limitations of a pre-modern society), wealth was established as well as a profane issue to be sought after and not a sacred gift from God. Wealth became private and could be used to divide a society instead of guaranteeing public prosperity.

At this historical point the age of the Prophets begins, fundamental critics of the factual conditions and reminders of the covenant. They radically opt for the demands of the poor. They criticise economical thinking (pre-capitalist) and stress social justice. The latter is even more important than observing the religious rituals, for action against social justice effectively means acting against the fundamental ideas of the covenant. The position of the prophets is thus a radical one; they refuse the idea that wealth could be used to create even more wealth as improper to fulfil social needs. This may be an explanation for the fact that their level of impact was always limited, no matter how famous their legacy remained within the Hebrew Bible.

Later generations, however, tried to incorporate the idea of growing wealth as a means to improve society. After the siege and destruction of Jerusalem and the loss of the Temple Judaism was forced both to conserve a past irrevocably lost and to adapt to the new circumstances of a Jewry living in exile among gentiles. The conservative part was the task of the compilers of the *Mishna*, the core of what later should emerge to be the Talmud. The Mishna tries to sketch rules and regulations to maintain the ritual obligations in an idealised state, as if the temple existed. It is meant to preserve a knowledge that must not be forgotten for when time comes, it will again be possible to uphold all these given commandments (Mitzwoth) in the land of Israel. Thus, it is not surprising that the Mishna still identifies wealth with land and everything that can be produced and harvested. It has no strong interest in money and is suspicious towards trade. Usury is strictly condemned and even the benefit of the seller falls under these regulations. The buyer is permitted to return the bought object if it is found to have been sold over a "standard price", ideally a price where no one loses and no one gains something, i.e. a game of zero sum. This is the logical result of a thinking that sets regulations for a sacred community that knows no separate spheres besides the religious one. The sin of exploitation by taking too much money for an object is called *ona'ah*.

Nevertheless, everything has two sides. Accordingly, in Talmudic times, the rabbis found these ideas of a sacred rural society inappropriate for their current living environment. As Jewish scholars, they had to find ways to adopt these laws to a changed society and define the above mentioned case of *ona'ah*. There is a tension between the needs of a complex society and the aim to view economy under mere religious conditions. Although self-interest is not valuated by the rabbis, they found ways to accommodate it and to interpret the religious law in a flexible way. The merchants of their times did not view self-interest as something fowl and the rabbis found ways to consider these views without abandoning the idea of *ona'ah*. What they could agree about was the idea of fair prices and the use of *ona'ah* as a means of price control. Prices could be deemed immoral even if both parties had already agreed upon them. What is more, rabbinic price control had a social dimension, i.e. a special interest in the caring for the poor. This means that the rabbis were well aware of economic laws and principles and could use this logic in order to be able to fulfil the covenant they were willing to maintain. We can identify smart innovations like Hillel's *prosbol*, a means of enabling monetary credits without infringing religious laws, thus supporting the economic prosperity of Israelite small merchants. The background of all innovations remains the idea of wealth as a sacred gift, of upholding the covenant facing a reality that demands economic logic and thus compromise. This flexibility is a basic feature of Talmudic and Rabbinic thinking in order to support and enlighten their religious communities as well as the not-so-religious every day life of their fellow Jews.

In the modern world of separated and autonomous realms self-interest and the laws of economy have gained a new dimension. This is also true for Jewish regards towards economy. Wealth, when it is no longer a zero-sum game, can positively contribute to immense social improvements as much as it may create the dark reverse side of human greed and exploitation. There are several ways of reacting to these altered circumstances within the Jewish community. Traditionalists would not give up the old concept of unseparated realms and the competence of religious authorities in economic questions. Others accept the separation of realms and try to update cold economic logic with Jewish thinking, which on the other hand creates the problem of facing a space were the inner logic of Jewish thinking has no value and must be imposed from the outside. A third party tries to rethink modern economy as a place where Jewish values can blossom, i.e. the invention of Jewish business ethics. This can bring together the yet separated realms without having one dominate the other. Wealth can thus remain a sacred gift without scorning economic need and thinking.

The Concept of Economy from a Christian Perspective

If one wishes to explore the concept of economy in a Christian perspective, he or she is to find a rather strange result. At first glance it seems like Christianity, or at least the Holy Scriptures of the New Testament, completely ignores the topic of economics. A sharp contrast to the Hebrew Bible or the Qur'an, where we find large passages dealing with economical questions. Things become clearer if we take into consideration that the Jesus-movement was an eschatological movement, eagerly awaiting the end of times and the Parousia. There was simply no need for trade and economics if the final judgement was at hand. However, this first glance is as misleading as the idea of a stark opposition of Christian thought and morals to economical ideas and currents. On the contrary, Christian thought has had a major impact on historical and recent concepts and theories of economics and on economy as such.

It must well be mentioned that "economy" in theological thought is a multi-layered term. It may describe the duties of a house-owner and the regulations of trade under the perspective of Christian ethics and believes. In a strictly theological sense, economy describes the divine economy, meaning God's ongoing communication and maintenance of his creation. The opposite is divine theology, a topic regarding the revelation of divine truths, a topic strictly limited to matters of faith and thus remaining a mystery, whereas divine economy has an understandable approach of communication that can be grasped. These two layers of economical understanding must be drawn into consideration when we deal with the concept of economy from a Christian perspective.

The origins of Christian economical thought were shaped by Greek influences, which dominated in the time of the formative Christian epochs. Thus the Greek concept of Oikonomia, or the maintenance of a household supervised by the house-owner, as Aristotle seminally formulated it, remained the benchmark for Christian economical thought among thinkers like Thomas Aquinas. Nevertheless, Aristotle does not believe in "capitalist" ideas of creating a surplus or lending money on interest. The main idea is to tread everything as economical that produces value, which excludes lending and mere trading.

A significant feature of both antique economy and Christian ethics is the question of slavery. Ancient world was unequivocally an epoch of slave labour and Christian believers and thinkers had to position themselves confronted with this fact. As already mentioned, Christian believers lived in the vein of an eschatological horizon. Waiting for a divine kingdom did render economic concerns a thing of a world and a logic surely to go by. However, the delay of the Parousia forced the young church to find answers to the pestering questions of their age. In Jesus Christ, all *status* of the former age are abandoned, the slave stands equally besides the freeman, women besides men, all are equally redeemed by their mutual believe in Jesus Christ. However, in this epoch this means a soteriological status, not a social one. Christianity refrains from social-revolutionary ambitions. The Apostle Paul leaves the institution of slavery untouched, reminding master and slave of their mutual dignity and their duty to treat each other as brothers. The ideal is surely to free the slave and not to accept any new slaves in the household, since Christians should not be the masters of other Christians, but it was no sooner as with Augustine of Hippo that we find a strong condemnation of slavery as a social institution that is surely to be eradicated in the end of times. Again, this is more a spiritual liberation than a social one.

It is this enduring spiritual understanding of liberation that made Christian thinkers of the Middle Ages accept the inequalities of the feudal system. The Christian teaching of the "two swords", i.e. the separation of a religious and a secular world allowed the distinction between a spiritual realm of equality and a world ruled by the logics of the mundane area. Even though Christianity was the major player of the medieval world, its mainstream currents did not consider social upheaval. Social inequalities were seen as a result of "natural law". It was in the reformatory age that undercurrents of social reform or revolt arose from areas long time untouched by official theological thought. Struggling with Lutheran orthodoxy, which again fostered social inequalities by its teaching of the "two regimes", reformers like Thomas Müntzer emphasised social-revolutionary concepts based on their new theological conceptions. The doctrine of human equality was enlarged towards a comprehensive and seemingly quite modern understanding of social justice. Unlike in modernity, these concepts were nevertheless connected to mythical and chiliastic movements and thoughts, ignoring the practical advantages of economical wisdom. The consequences for the followers of these movements were quite disastrous and the social revolution ended in blood.

Another important place where Christianity and economic wisdom combined were medieval monasteries. Monasteries following the rules of e.g. Benedict of Nursia or Francis of Assisi were *lieus* of social and economic progress and innovation apart from mainstream society. Until today the regulations are a source of practical wisdom and a blueprint for "good governance" and are the originators of such inevitable innovations as the double-entry bookkeeping. As times went by even the monasteries became rich, which on the other hand evoked monastic reform movements promoting the ideal of poverty.

An interesting economic and social innovation originating in monastic thought are the *"montes pietatis"*, predecessors of cooperative banks giving micro-credits to people normally standing outside the loan-system. They developed into 19th centuries' saving and associate banks, later on into the core of the emerging Christian social ethical thought and banking. Christian economics left the realm of the hereafter and settled in the immediate experience of everyday life. Pioneers of modern economic thought such as Adam Smith were both economists and philosophers that questioned the reign of natural law. Economics, both mundane and divine, could be lawful and thus a subject of modern scientific thought. This communication between the two realms enabled a transformation of religious, ethical concepts into concrete economical practice. Facing the urgent need for answers to the social question in the beginning of the industrial age and developing economic theories for peoples also and not just for people, Christian economic thought with its positive approach towards innovation (who can image an innovation greater than the Eschaton?) became a rich source of wisdom and an institution of correction towards the boundless excesses of early industrialised capitalism. Christianity maintained its critical approach towards materialism and consumerism just as secular economic theories maintained their critical approach towards Christianity. Concepts such as solidarity, subsidiarity and personality can be found both with religious and non-religious bedrocks and even if economic concepts were shaped in direct contrast to the system of Christian believes, their originators cannot deny that the origins of their thought are deeply influenced by a long history of western and thus Christian economic thought. The separation of the realms or "swords" is more or less abrogated, when it comes to voicing economic concerns and ideas. None other than the successors of St. Peter, the Popes, do not cease to publish encyclicals about social and economic issues, with Pope Francis just being the last in a line of pontifices like Leo XIII. (*rerum novarum*, 1891) or John Paul II. (*centesimus annus*, 1991). Francis just added a "green" colour to a well-known topic. This should not diminish the fact that most of the "work" regarding Christian social ethics is done by laypersons.

Christian commitment for social justice has long overcome mere charity and piety. The rise of democracy e.g. during the Weimar Republic enables Christian thinkers to directly or indirectly influence Christian politicians and parties, thus shaping the face of the young republic as well as the daily life of its workers. The implementation of social security systems cannot be imagined without these developments. Also after the cataclysmic events of the Second World War the impact of Christian Social Ethics on economic thought became decisive for the reality in post-war Western Europe with its focus on entrepreneur-responsibility and social partnership. These influences are measurable right until today.

Thus Christianity has undergone a long and multi-branched way of dealing with economics. From refraining from the thought of mundane economic duties in light of an immediately expected eschatological upheaval to medieval monastic innovations of economy and finance to finally shaping and confronting the world economic system, the concept of economy in Christianity is a challenging one as much as it is surprising.

The Concept of Economy from the Perspective of Islam

The tension between economy and economics and the question what their moral and legal fundament should be, is a contentious one. This is also true for Islam. On the other hand, Islamic thought of economy and economics has rules on its one and is sometimes to be seen as in contrast to established western conceptions of the two terms. It starts with the language. All basic terminology is in Arabic, the language of the Qur'an. This is not surprising since the fundamental principle of all Islamic thinking of economy and ecology is, like in all other concepts, the revealed word of God. Thus translations are always an approximation, but never an equivalent. As a result, many terms seem to correspond to well established western practices at first glance, but their religious connotation cannot be translated that easily. An example is the definition of usury in contrast to mere interest. Islamic teaching prohibits both whereas the translation of the Arabic term *ribā* is often quoted in the former case. The reason for this prohibition is reserved to the understanding of the faithful, in a sense, part of the overall religious struggle, which is known as *jihad*.

One of the mayor problems in drawing a picture of Islamic economics is the sheer variety of the Muslim countries worldwide and their range from extremely rich to extremely poor. Although Arabic is not the mother tongue of many Muslims, its scholarship and understanding is crucial to understand the Islamic approach towards all science such as economics. As a convenience, English is nowadays widely accepted as a language for negotiating transactions and financial products, even when the basis is still the original Arabic term. This sheds light on a fundamental problem when one endeavours to investigate Islamic economic thought. On the one hand, half of the scholars are trained in Arabic and the laws of Shari'ah, as well as the historical teachings of Muslim scholars on economic issues. However, their knowledge of classical western scientific approaches towards economics is but rather thin. On the other hand, well trained economic researchers with an academically background are often not used to read Arabic and seldom blessed with a profound knowledge of religious writing. The fruitful combination of the two types are a desideratum until today.

However, the source of all Islamic teaching on economics is the Qur'an and the Hadith. The Prophet himself was involved in trade, so the Qur'an has an overall positive approach towards trade, but values it under the predominance of spiritual among material outcome. The latter can lead to idolatry. Whereas the Qur'an and its teachings cannot be criticised, juridical thought, *fiqh*, can. As a result, economics are a part of *fiqh* and thus object of change and criticism.

Interestingly enough, no Muslim country in the world abandoned secular economic policies for religious policies, not even Afghanistan during the reign of the Taliban. However, at sector level many countries rely on *Shari'ah*-Boards to legitimate their financial and economic procedures. Thus a broad variety of Islamic banks, insurances and financial products could emerge.

The principals of Islamic economics in comparison to mainstream economic theory condemn the latter to be devoid of morals and a threat to the poor, which ignores the spiritual foundations of the goods God gave to man and the purpose of establishing a just society. This goes hand in hand with a new awareness of environmental issues. The core idea is that Allah has provided enough resources for a good life for everyone and is present in every act of the merchant. Islamic economics are thus orientated towards an ideal state. Trade as such and the market are seen as desirable, as long as they serve to support the spiritual wellbeing of the society, e.g. by guaranteeing the production of *halal* meat. Trade also helps connecting the Islamic world and serves to improve a society, whereas usury is seen as amoral.

All property ultimately belongs to God. However, Islam favours the idea of property and the concept of rent; investors may well earn profit from their investments, as long as the money is not earned with forbidden businesses, such as the production of alcohol or prostitution. Reimbursement, however, is not to be mistaken by interest. Interest remains strictly forbidden in all financial actions. *Shari'ah* deduction offers a wide range of market interventions if prices are seen as unjust. However, price control is only used scarcely in the Arab world, mostly to guarantee the supply with basic goods. The rules of the market are regarded with the conviction that abiding by the laws of *Shari'ah* guarantees prosperity and the survival of the statehood.

There have been several attempts for economic cooperation, but only few were successful, e.g. the Organization for Islamic Cooperation. The division of the Islamic denominations does note encourage a division towards economical question. An Islamic economy historically serves as a contrast point to capitalism and communism. In Iran, the entire banking system was transformed to be Shari'ah compliant. In other Muslim countries, Islamic banks compete with "classical" banks. This leads to the question what exactly "Islamic Banking" is, by far the most striking feature of Islamic economics in action. In the approximately seventy years since its establishment, the concept of Islamic banking has been a huge success. The basic principle is that the bank purchases imports or objects for the clients and re-sells these to the client for a profit mark-up. Thereby, no interest in produced. From these fundamental ideas a broad variety of financial products emerged. All these are Schari'ah-compliant, at least to the majority of legal schools. The financial product should include no forbidden fields of investment, such as pornography or the production of alcohol and pose no threat to the investor. Like generally in Islamic thinking about economics, the trade should serve the greater good of the community. On the Islamic stock markets, speculation is strictly condemned. Therefore, the religious obligation of giving *zakat* and the institution of *waqf*, a religious administration of land or buildings, are also part of economical thinking.

All in all, Islamic banking, financing and Islamic economical thinking are a rapidly growing fields of investigation by many scholars. The idea of applying well known secular structures to religious principles according to *Schari'ah* has been a huge success.

Common Features and Differences

If one tries to draw an overview comparison between the understandings of the key term "economy" within the three monotheistic religions Judaism, Christianity and Islam, one immediately notices similarities as well as differences. Let us begin with what interreligious dialogue must first start from: the things that unite.

In all three major religions of revelation, there are considerations on how to shape a trade pleasing to God, since they agree that wealth and property may not simply be excluded from the religious sphere. When looking at property, the focus can be on different things: While Judaism initially focused on land and livestock, capital was later added as a further element, which is also the focus of Christianity and Islam. But regardless of this emphasis, Judaism, Christianity and Islam assume that, just as man does not owe himself, man's private property and what he earns do not ultimately belong to him, but are to be understood as a divine gift. This means that property and wealth, because they are divinely bestowed, are not *eo ipso* condemnable, but they do give rise to an obligation. Just as human beings are called to communion with God and their fellow human beings, their possessions must also serve the common good and social justice, which excludes pure self-interest. Certainly, in the course of time, the economic sphere could also withdraw from the religious sphere, and sometimes even become independent, losing sight of the common good. This is particularly true of Christianity, where a so-called two-kingdom doctrine or two-swords doctrine often prevailed until modern times.

Although Islam is more open to trade than, for example, some Jewish currents, it also recognised the need to establish rules and norms to stop the misuse of property and trade. A rule found in Judaism as well as in Christianity and Islam is the condemnation and prohibition of usury as immoral. If all people owe their existence to the same God, this excludes the rule of people over people, living at the expense of others, i.e. exploitation and taking advantage of others. Although the prohibition of interest (on usury) is interpreted and handled with varying degrees of strictness in the three major revelatory religions, it is nevertheless clear that an unleashed capitalism cannot be legitimised religiously. Instead, for the sake of the dignity of all human beings and the mercy of God, Judaism, Christianity and Islam are inscribed with a social and diaconal commitment that focuses above all on the poor and socially disadvantaged.

All three monotheistic religions view and evaluate trade and property from a religious perspective and are therefore often critical when it comes to a purely profane economic thinking and world economic system geared towards maximising profits. This is especially true today, when the negative aspects of globalisation are becoming more and more apparent. Thus, starting from religious convictions, attempts are being made to create alternative economic forms and to ask how growing social injustice can be counteracted. Even if the search movement is not all in the same direction, it can be observed that all three religions are trying to conceptualise an economic ethic that is oriented towards the community and in which social responsibility is reflected.

Of course, there are not only parallels in attitudes towards business and financial activities between Judaism, Christianity and Islam, but also differences. Most striking are the different attitudes towards trade: While Islam is quite in favour of it, Judaism and Christianity originally viewed it with far more scepticism, which is certainly related to their respective histories. Judaism was initially a pastoral society; only in the course of the development of a centralised monarchy and economic changes did the lifestyle change and with it the attitude towards money. Although the Tanakh contains a prohibition of interest in several places, its observance and implementation varied, and in the course of the differentiation between Jews and non-Jews, a Jewish credit system developed in the Middle Ages.

Christianity, on the other hand, was initially filled with a determined expectation of the Parousia in the near future and, in the hope of the imminent return of Jesus Christ, did not attach any significant importance to earthly life, which is why the subject of interest is hardly ever addressed critically in the New Testament. Although there was a ban on interest in the early church, for centuries there was a tendency to distinguish the worldly realm from the spiritual realm, i.e. to differentiate between the throne and the altar. In modern times, due to the industrial revolution and the social question, the church had to deal in depth with the secular sphere, where the ban on interest was lifted from the 16th century onwards, which led to a Christian social ethic. Today, taking interest is no longer considered reprehensible in the Christian sphere, but usurious interest is.

The origins of Islam, on the other hand, are different. Inasmuch as Muhammad himself came from a merchant society and engaged in trade, there is no discernible tendency to distinguish between the religious and economic spheres, unlike in Christianity, for example. This is probably also connected to the fact that the question of interest is answered far less strictly in Christianity today than in Islam, where interest-bearing business and speculative transactions are rejected as harmful to the community and unethical. However, Islamic legal practice has always found ways to bring financial activities in line with the prohibition of interest. Thus, the economy prescribed by the Qur'an and the Shari'a is seen rather idealistically, as the image of an ideal state. Taking into account the Islamic prohibition of interest, an independent financial system is beginning to develop within the Islamic economic order (Islamic banking or Islamic finance), in which the principle of community benefit is in the foreground and banking transactions are attempted to be conducted according to the rules of Islam. Instead of working with interest, the idea of participation is emphasised, comparable to stock models.

Despite all the differences between religious ideas on the question of economy, one cannot help but notice that today a world economic system based on the interest system has de facto established itself in almost all countries of the world, regardless of which of the three great religions of revelation is influential in these countries.

List of Contributors and Editors

Moses L. Pava graduated from Brandeis University in 1981 and received his PhD from Ney York University's Stern School of Business in 1990. He is the former Dean of the Sy Sysm School of Business, Professor of Accountings and the Alvon Einbender University Professor of Business Ethics. His main topics are Jewish business Ethics, spirituality in business, and corporate accountability. He is a renowned lecturer, journal editor and author of many well received books such as Jewish Ethics In A Post-Madoff World, Business Ethics: A Jewish Perspective, Leading With Meaning, The Jewish Ethics Workbook, The Search for Meaning In Organizations, and Jewish Ethics As Dialogue.

André Habisch received his doctoral degree in catholic theology in 1993 at the University of Tübingen and finished his habilitation in 1998 at the University of Würzburg. Moreover, he completed a full study of Economics at the Free University of Berlin in 1992. In 1998, he became a Professor for Social Ethics and Social Policy at Catholic University Eichstaett-Ingolstadt. Since 2008, his main affiliation is at the Faculty for Business and Economics, where he coordinates the MA program 'Entrepreneurship and Innovation'. Since 1998, he serves as an Academic consultant of the Association of Catholic Entrepreneurs.

Rodney Wilson is currently an Emeritus Professor at Durham University. He served as an Economics Professor, specializing in Middle Eastern and Islamic Studies, and is the founder of the Islamic Finance Program. After retirement, he was a Visiting Professor at Qatar Faculty of Islamic Studies and the International Centre for Education in Islamic Finance in Kuala Lumpur. He is the author of numerous books and articles including a study of Jewish, Christian and Muslim Economic Thought published by Palgrave Macmillan

Christoph Böttigheimer has held the Chair of Fundamental Theology at the Catholic University of Eichstätt-Ingolstadt since 2002. He studied Catholic Theology at the universities of Tübingen and Innsbruck / Austria and obtained his doctorate at the University of Munich in 1993 and finished his habilitation in 1998 at the same University. He is the author of "Lehrbuch der Fundamentaltheologie", one of the most well-received and influential textbooks in the field of fundamental theology in the German-speaking world. His works in the ongoing legacy of the Second Vatican Council, on supplicatory prayer and core questions of faith have been translated into several languages. His most recent publication, besides a new and revised edition of the famous "Lehrbuch", is "Die Reich-Gottes-Botschaft Jesu. Verlorene Mitte christlichen Glaubens" (Herder, 2020) on Jesus' teaching in the Kingdom of God. He is member of many academic research and working committees, especially in the field of ecumenical dialogue and cooperation.

Wenzel Maximilian Widenka studied History, Catholic Theology and Interreligious Studies at the Universities of Bamberg and Vienna. He received his PhD in Jewish Studies at the University of Bamberg in 2019 with a study about the struggle for religious emancipation of 19th century Jews on the countryside. He is currently working as a research assistant for the Chair of Fundamental Theology of the Catholic University of Eichstätt-Ingolstadt. His most recent publications are "'*Sehet, da kommen Schakale, den Weinberg zu zerstören, den Weinberg Is-*

raels.' *Emanzipation und Konfessionalisierung im fränkischen Landjudentum in der ersten Hälfte des 19. Jahrhunderts*" (University of Bamberg Press, 2019), as well as "Seinen Namen heiligen, um das Volk zu retten", in: Bruns, Peter / Kremer, Thomas / Weckwerth, Andreas (Eds.): *Sterben & Töten für Gott? Das Martyrium in Spätantike und frühem Mittelalter* (Koinonia – Oriens), Münster 2022.

Index

Abu Ḥanafi 89
Accounting and Auditing Organization for Islamic Financial Institutions 77
Adam 53
Adrienne von Speyr 51
Aghion, Philipp 62
agriculture 6, 10
akribeia 52
al-Buchari, Muhammad Isma'il 74
Al-Sadr, Muhammad Baqir 91f.
Alawites 87
Angelus Silesius 51
Anthony of Padua 51
Aquinas, Thomas 45, 52, 61, 83
Arab Common Market 88
Arab League 88
ʿarboun 112
Aristotle 44–46, 49, 61, 133
Athanasius of Alexandria 51
Augustine of Hippo 49–52

bai bithaman ajil 90f.
baʿi madūm 112
Banisadr, Abohassan 93
Barnabas of Terni 57
basileia tou theou 47
ben Gamliel, Shimon 32f.
ben Shetach, Shimon 25–27, 29
ben Zakkai, Yochanan 19–21
Benedict of Nursia 55, 134
Benedict XVI. (Pope) 65
Bentham, Jeremy 78
Berman, Harold J. 56
Bernard of Clairvaux 51
Bernardino da Feltre 58
Birnbaum, Philipp 6f., 10
Böhme, Jakob 51
Boltzmann, Ludwig 61
Bonaventure 51
Boniface III (Pope) 53
Brandts, Franz 67f.
Brauns, Heinrich 66f.
brit 1f.

Catherine of Siena 51
Catholic Social Ethics 66
Chaney, Marvin 11
Chapra, Muhammad Umer 77f., 119
Charlemagne 52
Chiswick, Carmel Ullman 95
chrematistics 45
Christensen, Clayton 62
Christian Social Ethics 64f., 67, 69
church 49
community 27
Comte, Auguste 61
Constantinian turn 52
covenant 1–3, 8f., 11, 13, 15–18, 21, 25, 27f., 33, 35, 37f., 129f.
Covid-19 95

De Civitate Dei 49
de Yepes, Juan 51
divine economy 50f., 133
Domaine de Bargyius 88
double-entry book-keeping 56
Droste zu Vischering, Mary of the Divine Heart 51

ecology 136
economia 51
economics 33, 35f., 39, 45, 60f., 63, 65, 68, 71–74, 76f., 79, 81, 84, 89, 91, 96–98, 108, 119f., 129, 133f., 136f.
economy 5, 8, 10f., 13, 23, 25f., 28, 37, 43f., 46–53, 55f., 59–61, 63f., 68f., 71, 78, 91f., 129f 132f., 136, 140
Economy of Francisco 69
Eden 1
Edgeworth 61
El Najjar, Ahmed 98
Engels, Friedrich 63
environment 4, 36, 39

Feuerbach, Ludwig 63
fiqh 71, 75, 97f., 110, 136
First World War 66

Francis of Assisi 51, 134
Francis (Pope) 65
funds 76f, 92, 98, 105–109, 110-112.

gharar 103, 112
Goethe, Johann Wolfgang von 62
Gossen, Hermann Heinrich 46
Greenberg, Irving 21
Grundlach, Gustav 65

ḥadīth 74f., 119
ḥajj 76
ḥalā 111
ḥalāl 76, 82, 110
ḥaram 109
Harmèl, Leon 68
Hebrew Bible 6, 131f.
Hegel, Georg Wilhelm Friedrich 63
Hildegard of Bingen 51, 56
Hillel 33f., 132
ḥisbah 82f., 110
Hugh of St. Victor 51
ḥumash 2, 9
Hume, David 60f.
Hussein, Saddam 88, 91f.
Hutcheson, Francis 60

ibn Khaldun al Hadrami, Wali ad-Din Abd ar-Rahman ibn Muhammad 84f.
ibn Taimiya, Taqi ad-Din Ahmad 83
ibn Taymiya, Taqi ad-Din Ahmad 83
ijārah 100f., 111, 114–116
ijārah wa iqtīna 101
ijtimaʿ 104
interest *See* usury
islamic banking 92, 98, 109, 114, 119f., 140
Islamic Dawa Party 91
Islamic Development Bank 77, 89, 92, 96
Islamic Financial Services Board 77
Israel 2–4, 6, 8–11, 14–17, 20f., 31, 88, 95
istitnā' 115f.

jahalah 112
Jerusalem 47
Jesus 47
jihād 72

John of the Cross *Siehe* de Yepes, Juan
John Paul II. (Pope) 65, 135
John Scotus Eriugena 51
John VIII (Pope) 52
John XXIII. (Pope) 65
Jubilee Year 12
Judah 11, 15f.
Judas Iscariot 48
just price 83

kafala 104
ḳedushah 1f.
Khomeini, Ruhollah Musawi 93
Kleiman, Ephraim 24
Kuran, Timur 80

land 2f., 5, 8, 12f., 16
Laubach, Frank 51
Leo XIII. (Pope) 64, 135
Lubich, Chiara 51
Luther, Martin 51, 53–55, 129

mahdī 88
maisīr 112
Mandeville, Bernard 61
Marshall, Alfred 61
Martin of Tours 52
Marx, Karl 62f., 85
marxism 85
Maxwell, James Clerk 61
maysir 103
Mechthild of Magdeburg 51
Meister Eckhart 51
Merton, Thomas 51
Ministry of Islamic Affairs, *Daʿwa* and Guidance 75
mitsyot 2, 131
monarchy 12f., 15, 17f., 36
monastery 55f.
money 45
montes gratuiti 58
montes pietatis 57–59, 134
moral 71, 78, 83
muḍārabah 102f., 105, 110, 116
Müntzer, Thomas 54f., 134
murābaḥah 90, 100f., 111, 115

Murray, Andrew 51
mushārakah 101, 115 f.

Nasser, Gamal Abdel 87
Nell-Breuning, Oswald von 65
Neusner, Jacob 20, 22 f.
New Testament 47, 51, 69, 132, 139
Newton, Isaac 61
Nietzsche, Friedrich 62
nostra aetate 94

oikonomía 44–46, 133
ona'ah 23 f., 26, 29 f., 32, 131 f.
Onesimus 48, 59
Organization for Islamic Cooperation 88, 107, 137

Pacioli, Luca 56
Padre Pio of Pietrecina 51
Pareto, Vilfredo 61
Paton, Lewis 10
Paul (Apostle) 48 f., 59, 133
Paul VI. (Pope) 65
pe'ah 4, 7
Pesch, Heinrich 65
Philemon 48
Pilate, Pontius 47
Pius II (Pope) 52
Plotin 49
price control 30
prices 24 f., 29–32
prophet 14 f., 19, 21, 29
prosbol 33 f., 132
Pseudo-Dionysius the Areopagite 51

qarḍ ḥasan 98
quadragesimo anno 64
Qur'ān 71–75, 86, 111, 118 f., 132, 136, 140

Rabbah 27 f.
Reagan, Ronald 43
Reformation 53
regula Benedicti 56
rerum novarum 64
ribā 72, 76, 80, 91, 93, 98, 102, 106, 109, 111, 113, 117 f., 120, 136
Richard of St. Victor 51

Robbins, Lionel 79
Roman Empire 52, 54

Sacks, Jonathan 37
salam certificate 115
salam contract 111
Satlow, Michael 6
scarcity theory 79
Schumpeter, Joseph 62
Schütz, Roger 51
Second Vatican Council 94
Second World War 66, 68
self-interest 29 f.
sharī'a 71, 73–77, 79, 82 f., 85, 89 f., 93, 98 f., 102–114, 117, 120, 136 f, 138, 140
shī'ah 87–89, 91, 93
Shikra, Abba 19
Shiva 62
Sinai 1 f.
slavery 3 f., 48 f., 52, 68, 133
Smith, Adam 36, 60 f., 84, 134
Sombart, Werner 62
speculation 106
stewardship 50
subsidiarity 64
ṣukūk 103–105, 113–117
Summa Theologiae 45
sūra 72
sustainability 78

tabarru 104
takāful 77, 103–105, 116, 120
Tarfon (Rabbi) 29, 33
Tauler, Johannes 51
taxes 118
Teresa of Ávila 51
Thatcher, Margret 43
theologia 51
trade 82, 84, 86 f., 113, 139
translation 72

'*umra* 76
United Arab Republic 87
usury 2 f., 22 f., 72, 81 f., 93 f., 102, 113, 119, 130, 137–140
utilitarianism 78
utility theory 78

von Balthasar, Hans Urs 51
von Nell-Breuning, Oswald 65

wakala 105
Walzer, Michael 15
waqf 76, 118, 138

Washington consensus 43
wealth 1–4, 10, 12–18, 22f., 26, 28, 30, 33, 35–39, 129f
Weber, Max 43

zakāt 76, 117f.

www.ingramcontent.com/pod-product-compliance
Lightning Source LLC
Chambersburg PA
CBHW030556230426
43661CB00054B/2159